BUSINESS
OPPORTUNITIES

Vicki Hollett

Oxford University Press

Contents

5   Growth and Development   *page 46*

Topic	Language	Vocabulary / •Pronunciation	Skills Work
A career Finding things in common Past experiences Trvellers' stories	Past tenses: past simple, past continuous, and past perfect Present perfect with *for* and *since*	Verb-noun collocations • /d/, /t/ and /ɪd/ verb endings	*Speaking:* managing change *Listening:* a company history

6   Problem Solving   *page 56*

Topic	Language	Vocabulary / •Pronunciation	Skills Work
Making suggestions Considering possibilites A shrinkage problem Negotiating solutions Payment	Making and responding to suggestions First and second conditionals	Using a dictionary Payment vocabulary *to control* and *to check* • –'ll and –'d contractions	*Speaking 1:* negotiating tips *Speaking 2:* negotiating a deal

7   Telephoning to Exchange Information   *page 66*

Topic	Language	Vocabulary / •Pronunciation	Skills Work
Checking and correcting Documents Explanations Enquiries	Correcting wrong information Relative clauses Paraphrasing Indirect question forms	Business documents Verb-noun collocations • Spelling the alphabet	*Speaking:* placing an order *Reading:* insurance claims

8   Visitors   *page 74*

Topic	Language	Vocabulary / •Pronunciation	Skills Work
Polite phrases Showing interest Socializing Cultural differences	Requests, offers, thanks, invitations, and apologies Present perfect and past simple tenses (life experiences)	Expressions with gerunds Restaurant menu items • Polite intonation	*Speaking:* 'The Travel Game' *Listening:* a restaurant menu

Contents *(continued)*

TASKS

to introduce yourself to new business contacts

•

to exchange information about jobs and responsibilities

•

to discuss management styles and work methods

•

to set objectives for your English studies and plan how to achieve them

•

to describe a company's chain of command

PRESENTATION

I Read what these people have to say, then introduce yourself to other members of the class in similar ways.

Welcome to Tokyo. I'm Minoru Murofushi, the President of the Itochu Corporation, so I'm responsible for the overall performance of the group.

Bernd Setzkorn. Pleased to meet you. And this is Ferdinand Klatt. We work in Eberswalde. It's about thirty kilometres north-east of Berlin.

Hello. I'm Bernard Cazals, the Personnel Director of the Pernod Ricard Group. I'm based in Paris but I travel a lot.

2 🔊 Now listen to some more people meeting one another and make notes in the chart below.

	Conversation 1	Conversation 2	Conversation 3
Is this the first time they have met?			
Where do you think they are?			
What nationalities do you think they are?			

3 Look at these sentences from the conversations. Study the verb forms in **bold** print. For each one, say whether the speaker is talking about the past, the present, the future or a mixture of times. (Don't worry about the name of the tense – just think about the time.)

*Have you **been waiting** long?*
The speaker is talking about the past and the present.

1 Have you **been waiting** long?
2 How **was** the flight?
3 The meeting **starts** at three.
4 I **intend to** take you to your hotel first.
5 We're **going to** take a taxi.
6 We're **looking** for Bernd.
7 **Have** you **seen** him?
8 We **plan to** install a video suite in Milan.
9 He'll be happy to show you round when he **gets** back.
10 **Will** he be long?
11 We **met** at last year's conference.
12 I **live** here in Alicante.
13 **I'm leaving** tomorrow morning.
14 If you **had** more time, I'd take you sightseeing.
15 I **hope to** come back soon.

For information on English tense forms, see the Grammar and Usage notes on pages 170–188.

Good afternoon. I'm Lisa Schadewald. I work in the Shareholder Services Section of Minnesota Power in the USA. It's my job to answer questions from our shareholders and solve any problems they have.

How do you do? My name's Anke Rohland and I'm in charge of the welding department here at PCK in Schwedt. Let me introduce you to two of my staff …

LANGUAGE WORK

Getting acquainted   **1**   Work with a partner. Introduce yourself and get acquainted.

Find out
- their name
- where they come from

Find out about their company.
- Type of business
- Main customers
- Main competitors
- Locations

Find out about their job.
- Job title
- Department/Division
- Responsibilities

2   Now ask questions about your partner's past.

Find out
- how long they have had their job
- what job they had before this one
- about the last time they used English at work. (When was it? Who did they talk to or write to? What was it about?)
- where they have learnt English in the past

3   Ask about the future. Find out what your partner will need to do in English.

- Attend meetings (Who with?) (What about?)
- Make phone calls (Who to?) (What about?)
- Make presentations (Who to?) (What about?)
- Negotiate deals (What kind?) (Who with?)
- Show visitors around (Who?) (What will they show them?)
- Describe technical machinery or processes (What type?)
- Discuss figures (What kind?)
- Read (What?)
- Write (What?)
- Socialize (Who with?)

Executive titles   **1**   What job title do you have on your business card? Do you use different cards in different countries? A lot of executives do because job titles vary. Study this table to find out more.

Who's in charge here?

For travellers confused by the differing titles for top jobs around the world, here is a map to help you find your way around. It was compiled by a US executive recruitment agency, Paul Ray and Carre Orban International, and it compares North America's relatively consistent job titles with the strange mixture used in Europe.

FUNCTION	FRANCE	GERMANY	SPAIN	UK	US
To act as Honorary Spokesperson for an association (not a company).		Präsident			
To direct the actions of the advisory board (no operating responsibility).	Président du Conseil	Ehrenvorsitzender / Vorsitzender des Aufsichtrates	Presidente Honorario	Honorary Chairman	
To organize and lead the board. To develop and maintain the definition of the board's role.	Président Directeur Général; Gérant	Sprecher des Vorstandes (AG); Vorsitzender der Geschäftsführung (GmbH)	Presidente del Consejo de Administración	Chairman	Chairman
To take the final responsibility for profits. To establish long and short term objectives, plans and policies and implement them. To co-ordinate operations between divisions and departments. To represent the company with major customers, the financial community and the public.	Président Directeur Général; Gérant	Vorsitzender des Vorstandes (AG); Geschäftsführer (GmbH)	Director General	Managing Director	Chief Executive Officer
To assist the top executive in directing, administering and co-ordinating company operations, personnel, financial performance and growth.	Directeur Financier		Subdirector General		Chief Operating Officer
To be accountable for the company's overall financial plans and policies.	Directeur Financier et Gestion	Finanzvorstand (AG) Finanzgeschäfts-führer (GmbH)	Director Financiero	Financial Director	Chief Financial Officer
To be responsible for the company's accounting practice.	Directeur Financier et Trésorier	Leiter des Rechnungswesens	Jefe de Contabilidad		Controller
To be responsible for the company's relationships with financial institutions.		Finanzdirektor	Tesorero		Treasurer
To manage a division of a company.	Directeur Général; Directeur; Directeur Adjoint	Geschäftsführer	Director General	Managing Director	President

2   Was your country mentioned in the table? What job titles do your executives and managers have? Can you translate them into English?

3   Highlight or underline all the verbs (actions) in the table that describe jobs and responsibilities. Then give a short description of your job, using as many of the verbs as you can.

Management styles

I Have you ever heard of Richard Branson? Read this article about the way he works. Is there anything unusual about his management style? Do you think you would like to work for him?

Richard Branson's

10 SECRETS OF SUCCESS

Richard Branson became famous as a 'hippy' businessman in the 1960s when he set up a record company. Today he runs the successful Virgin airline and he's still breaking many of the traditional rules of management. So how does he do it?

1. He regularly works an eleven-hour day, starting around eight and finishing around seven at night.

2. He spends a lot of time talking to people on the telephone but he never sends memos.

3. He rarely holds board meetings. He makes decisions on the phone or on the tennis court.

4. He has a good memory and he writes people's names on his hand so he doesn't forget them.

5. He invites every single one of his 10,000 employees to a party at his home in Oxfordshire every year. The last party cost around £100,000.

6. He continually questions his employees about every aspect of the business and he tries to pick holes in their arguments to find out whether their ideas will work.

7. If he becomes annoyed in meetings, he leaves the room. He hardly ever loses his temper.

8. He employs people he likes personally. This is more important to him than qualifications.

9. He has had several business failures in the past and nearly went bankrupt several times but he has always survived. He puts his success down to good ideas, good people, and good luck.

10. He didn't go into business to make money. He went into business because he wanted a challenge.

2 Work with a partner. Look at the facts about Branson and ask and answer questions about how he works. Use these question forms to help you.

What ...?   How ...?   How many ...?
Where ...?   Does he ...?   How much ...?
When ...?   Has he ...?   What sort of ...?
Why ...?   How often ...?

3 Now ask your partner similar questions about the way they do their job.

Time management **I** In a busy working day, it's not easy to find time to study. Discuss these questions with your teacher and classmates and plan how to manage your time.

1 Which part of your day is the most productive? When do you find it easiest to concentrate and when do you find it most difficult?
2 When do you find time to relax?
3 When will you find time to study English?
4 How do you plan to study English between lessons? Are you going to
   • read English newspapers?
   • work with this coursebook?
   • read English books?
   • watch English programmes on TV?
   • watch English films at the cinema or on video?
   • listen to English radio programmes?
   • listen to English cassettes in your car?
   • do anything else? (What?)

2 Now set yourself some objectives for your English studies. Complete these sentences.

I'm going to _____ .
I plan to _____ .
I intend to _____ .
I'd like to _____ .
I hope to _____ .

Which of the phrases sound most definite?

Jobs Quiz

1 Is your job the right job for you? Find out by doing this quiz. Work in pairs. Tick the statements your partner agrees with.

1 I'd love to do a parachute jump.
2 I don't like telling other people what to do.
3 I prefer spending time on my own rather than in a crowd.
4 I find it easy to set myself objectives.
5 I have difficulty making decisions.
6 I find it difficult getting to know new people.
7 I'd love to travel abroad.
8 Friends sometimes complain that I order them around.
9 I like to have the advice and support of people more experienced than myself.
10 I don't like volunteering opinions in case they are unpopular.
11 I like to try to find new solutions to old problems.
12 I would prefer to be team captain than team member.
13 I get embarrassed easily.
14 I don't mind where I go with my friends as long as they are happy.
15 I like the latest fashions.
16 I like to be fully responsible for anything that I do.

2 Now add up your ticks and check your scores. Three or four ticks in any category indicates personality characteristics you should take account of when choosing a job.

Scoring

A	1	7	11	15
B	2	5	9	14
C	3	6	10	13
D	4	8	12	16

Personality types

A Characteristics	**B Characteristics**	**C Characteristics**	**D Characteristics**
The entrepreneur	*The team worker*	*The backroom worker*	*The leader*
Your are the adventurous type. You enjoy new challenges and taking risks. You could find success in stock market dealing rooms or anywhere you can put your flashes of genius to good use.	You work well with others but dislike having responsibility for other people, preferring to implement other people's plans rather than your own. You would probably do well in the armed forces or the Civil Service.	You are a little shy, and find it difficult to mix with new people. You would do well in any behind-the-scenes job where you don't have to come face to face with strangers every day, such as a researcher or librarian.	You are confident in your abilities and you prefer to be in charge rather than to take orders. You enjoy having lots of people around you and would do well in a managerial post or any job which involves selling.

Employment | Match the verbs (actions) in the box with one of the Employment Roads (1–6). Three have been done for you.

retire	take on staff	recruit staff
resign *Road 2*	dismiss staff *Road 6*	make staff redundant
sack staff *Road 6*	be unemployed	hand in your notice
receive a pension	fire staff	

2   Now ask a partner some questions about their employment.

- Find out if they have ever been unemployed or made redundant.
- Ask them about their retirement plans.
- Find out how much notice they must give if they want to resign.
- Ask whether they are ever involved in taking on new staff.
- Find out if they have ever had to sack someone.

SKILLS WORK

Speaking

I A colleague from one of your foreign subsidiaries is being seconded to your place of work for three months. They will become your assistant, helping you in your day-to-day work. Write a list of people in your organization that they will need to know.

2 Work with a partner. Take it in turns to introduce your new assistant to their job.

1 Explain what they will be responsible for.
2 Show them the list and tell them who the people are. (Explain their job titles and responsibilities.)
3 Give any background information that might be helpful.

He has worked here for twenty years. He started in sales and moved over to marketing.
She deals with international accounts but she also knows a lot about the computer system.

Listening

I Schering is an international company engaged in agricultural and pharmaceutical activities. The French pharmaceutical subsidiary has recently changed its organizational structure. Listen to a manager describe the new structure to some colleagues from other parts of the organization and complete the organigram.

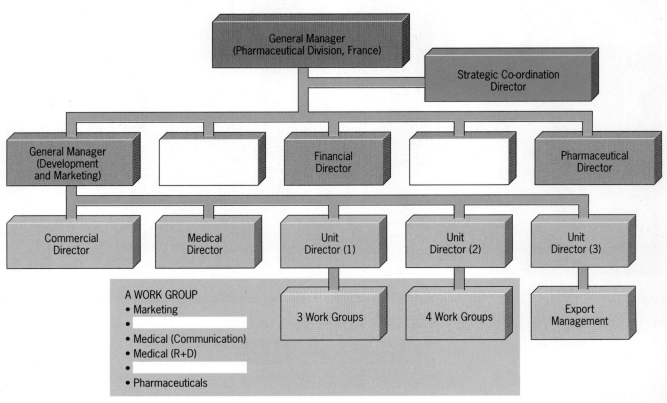

2 📼 Listen again and answer these questions.

1 Which person on the chart made the presentation?
2 Who does he report to?
3 What are the Unit Directors responsible for?
4 What three advantages of the work groups does he mention?

3 Work in groups of three or four. Describe the structure of your organization (or your part of the organization) as you would to visitors from abroad. Draw an organigram, say who is responsible for what and explain the reasons for the structure.

Pronunciation 📼 Listen to these words from the manager's presentation. For each word, mark the syllable where the main stress falls.

Example: organization.

1 general
2 director
3 production
4 personnel
5 responsible
6 advantages
7 motivating
8 responsibility
9 development
10 expertise

Now try saying the words yourself. Make sure you stress the right syllable.

OBJECTIVE

to make and change arrangements over the phone

TASKS

to discuss changes to an itinerary for a visit

•

to make contact over the phone

•

to make appointments

•

to make changes to schedules for visits and meetings

•

to organize a conference programme

PRESENTATION

1 📼 You are going to hear three telephone calls about the itinerary below. Listen and make any necessary changes.

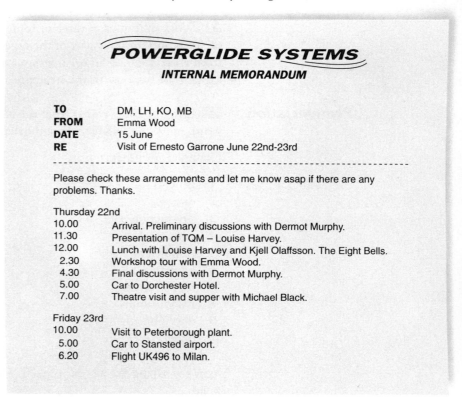

POWERGLIDE SYSTEMS
INTERNAL MEMORANDUM

TO	DM, LH, KO, MB
FROM	Emma Wood
DATE	15 June
RE	Visit of Ernesto Garrone June 22nd-23rd

- -

Please check these arrangements and let me know asap if there are any problems. Thanks.

Thursday 22nd

10.00	Arrival. Preliminary discussions with Dermot Murphy.
11.30	Presentation of TQM – Louise Harvey.
12.00	Lunch with Louise Harvey and Kjell Olaffsson. The Eight Bells.
2.30	Workshop tour with Emma Wood.
4.30	Final discussions with Dermot Murphy.
5.00	Car to Dorchester Hotel.
7.00	Theatre visit and supper with Michael Black.

Friday 23rd

10.00	Visit to Peterborough plant.
5.00	Car to Stansted airport.
6.20	Flight UK496 to Milan.

2 📼 Here are some extracts from the three conversations. Supply the missing words or phrases, then listen again to check your answers.

Conversation 1

Operator	Powerglide Systems.
Ernesto	I'd like to speak to Emma Wood.
Operator	_____ ?
Ernesto	Ernesto Garrone.
Operator	One moment. I'll _____ .
...	
Emma	Was there _____ ?
Ernesto	No, that's everything, I think.
Emma	_____ if there's anything else we can do.
Ernesto	Thank you.
Emma	_____ Thursday at around eleven, _____ .
Ernesto	Yes, I'm looking forward to _____ .
Emma	Thank you for _____ . Goodbye.

Conversation 2

Kjell Could we meet on Friday instead?

Emma He's _____ the Peterborough plant.

Kjell I know, but _____ a breakfast meeting?

Emma Yes, that _____ be possible.

Kjell _____ 8.30 at the Dorchester?

Emma Yes, OK.

Conversation 3

Emma Mr Garrone _____ a colleague — a Mrs Agnelli. Would you mind _____ her the rolling mill in operation?

Michael No, _____ .

Emma That's very good of you.

Michael When _____ you best?

Emma Some time on Thursday, if possible. _____ the morning or afternoon?

Michael The afternoon, I think.

3 We often use the word *would* when we are making arrangements. Match the two halves of these sentences from the conversations.

1	Would you mind if I ...	**a**	put it on the schedule then?
2	She'd like to ...	**b**	arrange a demonstration?
3	Would you like me to ...	**c**	very kind.
4	That would be ...	**d**	have a look at your rolling mill.
5	Would you ...	**e**	brought a colleague with me?
6	Would you mind ...	**f**	showing her the rolling mill?
7	Would you prefer ...	**g**	the morning or the afternoon?

4 We often use the present continuous tense to talk about planned future arrangements.

Mr Garrone is bringing a colleague.
I'm not arriving until eleven.

And we use the past continuous to talk about previous plans.

We were going on a workshop tour at 2.30, but I can put that off.

Work with a partner. Ask and answer questions about Mr Garrone's itinerary.

A *When's he arriving?*
B *He was arriving at ten, but now he's coming at eleven.*
A *And what's he doing first?*

LANGUAGE WORK

Polite questions

1 Study this conversation. Does B agree to A's request or refuse?

A *Would you mind if I opened the window?*
B *No, not at all.*

2 Work with a partner to ask and answer questions. Use the correct question form from the box.

Would you ...?	*Would you like to ...?*
Would you mind ...?	*Would you like me to ...?*
Would you mind if I ...?	*Would you prefer ...?*

1 Ask for permission to use your client's phone.
2 Find out whether your guest wants tea or coffee.
3 Offer to call a taxi for your visitor.
4 Invite your partner to play golf with you next week.
5 Ask your supplier to make you a copy of their new price list.
6 Ask your colleague to give you a lift to the airport.

Starting and finishing calls

1 We use a lot of standard phrases to start and finish telephone calls.
Make yourself a checklist for future reference. Study the table below then add these phrases.

Anyway ...	*I'll look forward to seeing you on Tuesday, then.*
How are things?	*Let me know if there's anything I can do.*
I'm phoning to ask ...	*Thank you for calling.*

Welcoming the call	Nice to hear from you.
Polite enquiries	How are you?

Saying why you're phoning	The reason I'm phoning is ...

Indicating you're ready to finish	Right then ...

Offering help	Give me a ring if you have any problems.

Confirming future plans	See you on the 26th, then. Until Friday, then.

Ending on a friendly note	Thanks for your help.

	Have a nice day.

2 Now complete the beginning and ending of the conversation below. Use words and phrases from the table.

The start
A Sandra Parker.
B Hello Sandra, Hans Grass here.
A Hans. _____ . _____ ?
B I'm fine, thanks. _____ with you?
A Not bad at all, thanks.
B Sandra, _____ if you have the details for the multimedia meeting.

The finish
A _____ .
B Yes, I'll do that. Thanks.
A _____ . _____ Friday, then.
B Yes. _____ .
A You're welcome. _____ .

Telephone quiz Work with a partner. Test yourself with this quiz.

How efficient do you sound on the phone?
Can you impress foreign callers with your telephone English?
Find out by doing this quiz.

1 Think of another way of saying
a I'll connect you.
b Just a minute.
c The line's busy.

2 Explain these words:
a a code
b an extension

3 You hear the following expressions on the phone. What do you think the speakers mean?
a You're very faint.
b He's tied up at the moment.
c Could you read that back to me?
d Can you bear with me for a second?
e I'll get back to you first thing on Monday.

4 Choose the polite reply in each of these conversations.

a **Can I speak to Loretta?**	c **This is Terry Rance.**	e **Would morning or afternoon suit you best?**
1 Who are you please?	1 Sorry?	
2 Who's calling please?	2 Repeat, please.	1 I don't mind.
		2 I don't care.
b **Could I have your name please?**	d **Is she free on Friday?**	f **Is that everything?**
1 Yes, I'm Anna Long.	1 No, she isn't.	1 Yes, of course.
2 Yes, it's Anna Long.	2 I'm afraid not.	2 Yes, that's the lot.

Making appointments

1 Work with a partner. One person is the caller (white boxes) and the other person is everyone else: a switchboard operator (green boxes), a secretary (yellow boxes), and the person receiving the call (blue boxes). Follow the arrows to make as many different calls as you can.

2 Now close your books and act out some similar calls.

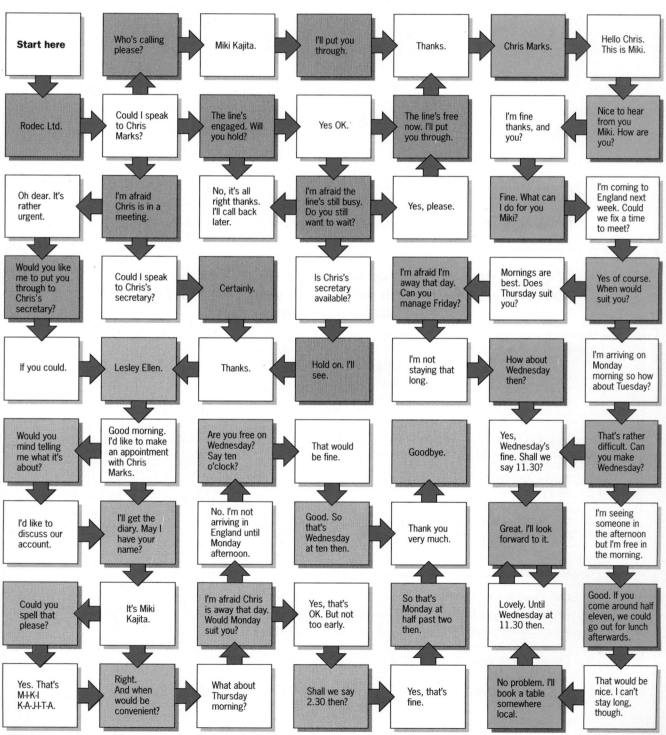

Pronunciation

/s/ see   /θ/ thirty
/z/ Thur<u>s</u>day   /ð/ <u>th</u>en

I   Listen to these words and repeat. Notice the position of your tongue.

months   thanks   thinks   something   sixth

2   Listen to this conversation, then practise it with a partner.

A   *See you on Thursday at three-thirty, then.*
B   *Thursday the sixth?*
A   *No, Thursday the thirteenth.*
B   *OK. See you on Thursday the thirteenth at three-thirty, then. Thanks.*

Changing arrangements

I   Put the sentences in this conversation into the correct order. Number the boxes. Then read it with a partner to check your answers.

☐ Yes, it's off. It was OK for me, but Christophe has got to go to the States.
☐ OK. I'll pencil it in and wait to hear from you, then.
☐ I don't know. I'll get in touch with him and find out.
☐ Has something come up, then?
1 Claudia Cavosi
☐ I was going to London, but I could put it off.
☐ Could we? Would the Wednesday of the week after suit you?
☐ Claudia, this is Heinrich. Bad news about next week's meeting, I'm afraid.
☐ Thanks, Claudia. Sorry to put you out like this.
☐ Yes, I'll get back to you as soon as I can.
☐ It's no problem. Can Christophe make it, though?
☐ He's a difficult man to pin down, isn't he? Do you want to fix another time?

2   Think of another way to say the sentences below. Use these multi-word verbs from the conversations above.

to put someone out   *to get in touch with someone*
to put something off   *to come up*
to be off   *to pin someone down*
to pencil something in

1   Could we write a provisional date in our diaries?
2   I'm sorry to upset your plans like this.
3   I'm afraid the conference is cancelled.
4   Something unexpected has happened and I can't make it.
5   We'll have to delay the meeting.
6   I can't make them decide exactly what they're going to do.
7   I need to contact my lawyer.

SKILLS WORK

Listening   **1**   ▭ Two people are discussing arrangements for a conference. Look at the information on the facilities available at the conference centre. Tick all the points they mention.

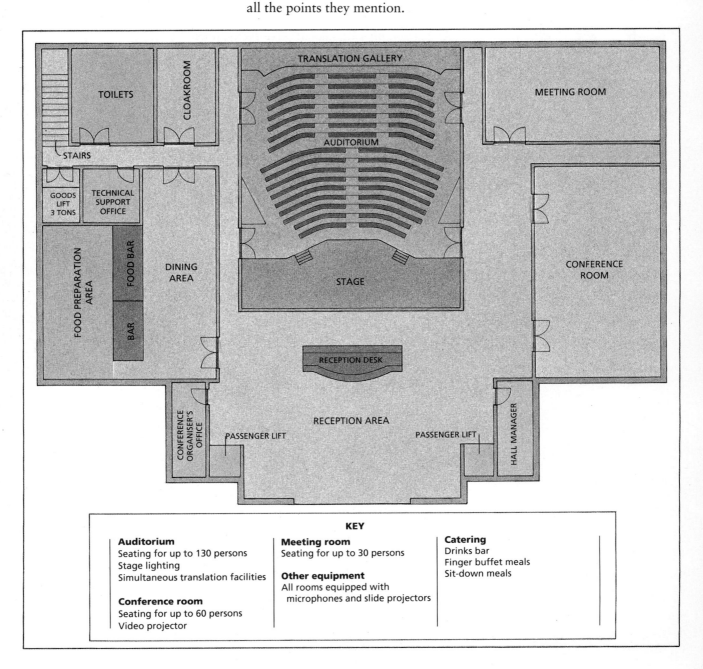

KEY

Auditorium
Seating for up to 130 persons
Stage lighting
Simultaneous translation facilities

Conference room
Seating for up to 60 persons
Video projector

Meeting room
Seating for up to 30 persons

Other equipment
All rooms equipped with
 microphones and slide projectors

Catering
Drinks bar
Finger buffet meals
Sit-down meals

2   ▭ Listen again if necessary and answer these questions.

1   Why can't the speakers sort out the programme now?
2   How many people are attending Mr Tanaka's talk?
3   What time is the conference starting and why?
4   What do they arrange to do?

Speaking 1   Work with a partner. You are going to plan the schedule for the first day of an international sales conference. One person should look at the information below and the other should look at the information in File 3 on page 151.

You have booked the conference venue. Phone your colleague at head office, find out how many delegates would like to attend each presentation and complete the programme. Use the information about the conference centre from the key to the brochure on the opposite page, and the list of speakers below.

Speakers
Mr Tanaka (Japan)
Dr Joeckel (Germany)
Ms Bocage (France)
Mr Alatali (Turkey)
Ms Kirmanen (Finland)
Mr Lucerni (Italy)
Ms Morey (USA)

Programme (DAY 1)	Session 1 (9.00-10.30)	Session 2 (11.00-12.30)	Session 3 (2.00-3.30)
Auditorium	Mr Tanaka		
Conference Room			
Meetings Room			

Speaking 2   Work with a partner. One person should use the information below and the other should look at the information in File 1 on page 150.

1   You work at the headquarters of an international company. You are spending next week at your UK subsidiary in London and you have to arrange a meeting with the UK Sales Director to discuss next year's targets. You'll probably need two or three hours of their time. Phone and fix an appointment. Use your diary.

2   The Sales Director calls you back ten minutes later. Take the call.

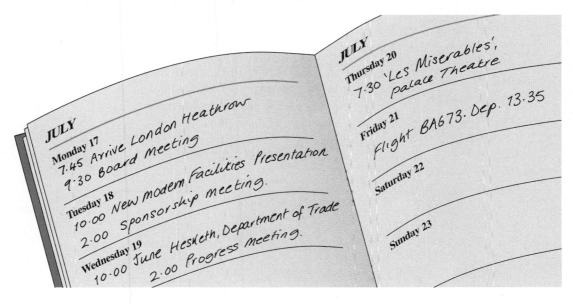

JULY

Monday 17
7.45 Arrive London Heathrow
9.30 Board meeting

Tuesday 18
10.00 New modern Facilities Presentation
2.00 Sponsorship meeting.

Wednesday 19
10.00 June Hesketh, Department of Trade
2.00 Progress meeting.

JULY

Thursday 20
7.30 'Les Miserables', Palace Theatre

Friday 21
Flight BA673. Dep. 13.35

Saturday 22

Sunday 23

OBJECTIVE

to exchange information about the activities of business organizations

TASKS

to follow a company presentation

•

to exchange numerical data

•

to ask for information about foreign companies

•

to predict the role of organizations in the future

•

to describe the structure of a business organization

•

to compare corporate cultures

PRESENTATION

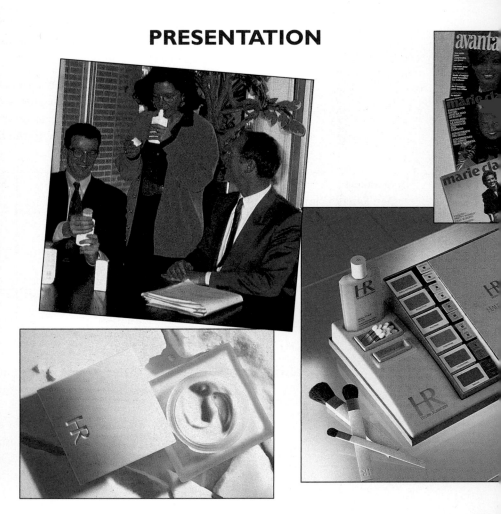

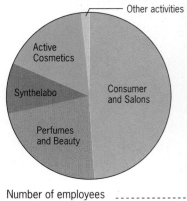

1 You are going to hear a manager from L'Oréal talking about her company. Before listening, find out if your colleagues know anything about L'Oréal's business activities.

2 Listen to the description of the company's activities and complete the pie chart and notes with the correct figures.

Turnover	FFr (bn)	%
Consumer and Salons		
Perfumes and Beauty		
Synthelabo		
Active Cosmetics		
Other activities		

Sales breakdown by division

Other activities

Active Cosmetics

Synthelabo

Consumer and Salons

Perfumes and Beauty

Number of employees _ _ _ _ _ _ _ _ _ _

Gross turnover _ _ _ _ _ _ _ _ _ _

3 🔲 Listen again and complete these extracts from the presentation. Use one word per space.

1 We have production _____ , _____ and _____ in all five continents.

2 ... the largest part of our _____ comes from Consumer and Salons activities.

3 Here we have an exceptional _____ of prestigious _____ which includes Lancôme, Helena Rubenstein, and Biotherm.

4 ... this division has dual objectives: firstly to develop new, technically-advanced cosmetics, and secondly to _____ our close relationships with pharmacists — a key _____ of _____ .

5 Synthelabo is making _____ in the treatment of central nervous system disorders at the moment, and it will become a world _____ in this _____ in the future.

6 ... we _____ a major _____ in the Marie-Claire publishing group ...

4 Now make similar sentences about your company. Describe

- the locations you operate in
- where the largest part of your turnover comes from
- the range of products/services you offer
- the role of your division or department
- one of your current projects and your future plans
- any other points of interest.

LANGUAGE WORK

Pronunciation

1 ▭ Listen to ten short conversations and write down all the numbers, dates, and times you hear.

2 Practise saying these different kinds of numbers aloud.

For information on how to pronounce numbers, see the Grammar and Usage notes on page 182.

3 Now write down lots of numbers that are relevant to you. They can be any numbers you like: your shirt size, your bank account number, the date of your wedding anniversary, etc.

Dictate the numbers to some colleagues. They should write them down, then guess what the numbers are.

Collecting information

1 Work with a partner. Ask and answer these questions about AT&T.

What are AT&T's principal business activities?
Where is their head office located?
What are their total revenues?
What is their net income?
How many employees do they have?
What are their current projects?

Think of other similar ways of asking each question.

What are AT&T's main activities?
What do AT&T do?
What products or services do AT&T sell?

	Principal business activities	Head Office	Total revenues	Net income	Number of employees	Current projects
AT&T	The provision of telecommunications services and communications equipment	Avenue of the Americas, New York	$ 64,904m	$3,807m	312,700	- Developing the world's first full-colour videophone - Building a $17m undersea fibre-optic cable system in the Caribbean

2 Work with a partner. One person should look at the information below. The other should look at the information in File 5 on page 152.

1 Use the information on Robert Bosch GmbH to answer your partner's questions.

	Main business activities	Location of headquaters	Total sales	Gross margin	Number of employees	Current projects
Robert Bosch GmbH	The production of automotive equipment, communications technology and consumer goods	Stuttgart, Germany	DM 31,824m	DM 560m	179,636	- Opening more offices in Eastern and Central Europe - Expanding their development and manufacturing network abroad - Introducing Total Quality Management systems

2 Your partner has some information on Komatsu. Ask questions about
- the company's principal business activities
- where the head office is based
- the company's turnover and profit
- the number of employees
- the company's current projects.

3 When you have finished, ask similar questions to find out more about your partner's own company.

Future predictions

In a changing world, new ideas are influencing the workplace. Read what these four business school students say about the organizations of the future and answer the questions.

1 Which student thinks

1 businesses will become less hierarchical?
2 there will be less unemployment?
3 the state will provide fewer services?
4 there will be less prejudice and society will become more equal?

 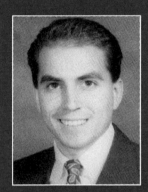  

'In years to come, declining birth rates and consequently smaller numbers entering the work force, will make labor scarce. Job sharing and part-time workers will become far more commonplace.'

**Vivek Sood,
Hautes Etudes
Commerciales, France**

'The glass ceiling will be broken as women and minorities finally take their rightful place in upper management; no longer will a Who's Who of business leaders be an array of white male faces.'

**Ted Ochs,
Fuqua School of Business,
Duke University, Durham,
North Carolina, USA**

'The distinction between leaders and their subordinates is diminishing. The corporation of the future will be less bureaucratic, more entrepreneurial, more flexible and more creative. The structure will be leaner and flatter.'

**Peter Vestergaard Larsen,
Copenhagen Business School,
Denmark**

'In the 21st century, the majority of the population will be dissatisfied with the quality and delivery of government services. Multinational corporations will assume the current role of government and help to forge a new world order. Social security, police forces, health care and education will all be provided by the private sector.'

**Richard Dantas,
The Wharton School,
University of Pennsylvania, USA**

Source: Air France and *Fortune* Magazine, 1992

2 Look at Vivek Sood's predictions again and find words which mean the opposite of

1 rising ....
2 plentiful ....
3 unusual ....
4 full-time ....

3 Look at Ted Ochs' predictions again and find words and phrases which mean

1 the name of a book that lists well-known or powerful people.
2 small social groups.
3 an invisible barrier.
4 a collection, a display.
5 morally correct, proper.

4 Complete this table with words from Peter Vestergaard Larsen's predictions.

noun	adjective
bureaucracy	------------------------------------
entrepreneur	------------------------------------
flexibility	------------------------------------
creation	------------------------------------

5 Match the words that went together in Richard Dantas's predictions. The first one has been done for you.

1 government   a care
2 multinational   b forces
3 private   c services
4 health   d security
5 social   e sector
6 police   f corporations

6 Work with a partner. Find out which future predictions they agree with, and which ones they like.

A *Do you think labour will become scarce?*
B *No, I don't, but I think there'll be more job sharing.*
A *Do you like that idea?*
B *Yes. It'll be good if more people have the option of working part-time.*

7 What do you think the business world will be like in the twenty-first century? Try writing your own predictions about the future. You might like to consider one of these issues.

• the Third World
• the role of banks
• the use of computers
• ecology and the environment
• your children's employment prospects

RECORDING VOCABULARY

1 It is important to record new English words so you can review them later. How do you usually record new vocabulary? Have you got a vocabulary notebook? Do you store new words alphabetically or by topic headings?

> **M**
> minorities
> majority
> multinational

> <u>ORGANIZATIONS</u>
> bureaucracy
> hierarchy
> multinational

Do you store new English words in a file on your computer? Do you store words on vocabulary cards?

2 There are several different ways of recording meanings or definitions.

- You can write the word in your own language.

> a range –
> une gamme

> commonplace –
> alltäglich

- You can draw a diagram or picture.

> hierarchy △

> declining ↘

- You can write an English explanation.

> glass ceiling –
> an invisible barrier

> minorities –
> small social groups

- You can explain with an opposite.

> declining –
> opposite of rising

> scarce –
> opposite of plentiful

- You can write an example sentence.

> You have to go through a complex <u>bureaucratic</u> procedure if you want to get your money back.

> He only works 18 hours a week. He's a <u>part-time</u> worker.

3 Don't forget to note the pronunciation of a word if you think it may be difficult to remember.

> hierarchy –
> /ˈhaɪərɑːkɪ/

> multinational –
> ■■□■■

4 Words are easier to remember if they are recorded in groups. You could record common word partnerships and word families in tables or networks.

Word partnerships	
multinational	corporations
social	security
police	force
health	care
private	sector

Noun	Adjective	Verb	Person
creation	creative	to create	creator
bureaucracy	bureaucratic	–	bureaucrat
organization	organized	to organize	organizer
production product	productive	to produce	producer

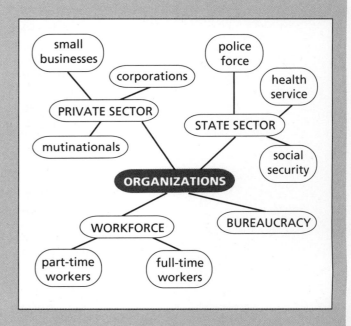

SKILLS WORK

Speaking **I** Here are three diagrams representing the structure of an organization. Look at diagram 1. Which group of people

1 own the company?
2 sell to the company?
3 formulate policy?
4 buy from the company?
5 work for the company?

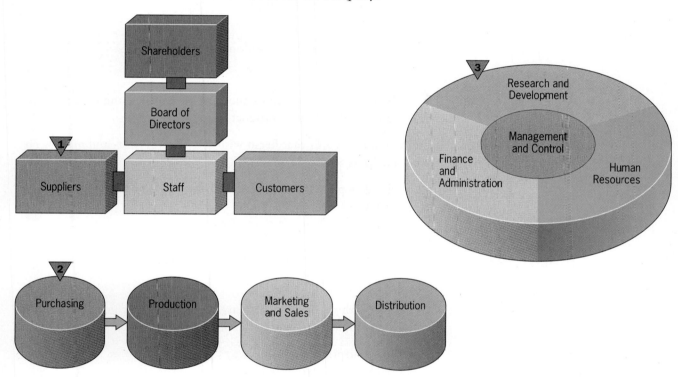

2 Look at diagrams 2 and 3. Which part of this organization

1 manufactures the products?
2 sells the products?
3 deals with personnel matters?
4 creates new products?
5 buys supplies?
6 gets the products to the consumers?
7 records transactions, collects cash, makes payments, and calculates costs?
8 plans, schedules, monitors, measures, and gives direction?

3 Do any of these diagrams represent the structure of your organization? How are they similar? How are they different? Draw a diagram of your organization and explain it to another student.

Reading   **1**   You are going to read an article about Microsoft, the US software producer. Do you know anything about this company?

2   Would you like to work for Microsoft? Read the article on the opposite page and find out.

3   Note down some questions about the article.

Why do they understaff their product teams?
What's the pay like?

Then ask a colleague your questions and answer theirs.

4   Microsoft employees think they are **over**worked and the company deliberately **under**staffs its product teams.

Think of more words that begin with the prefixes *over-* and *under-*. Here are some ideas to get you started.

- to charge a price that's too high or low
- too heavy or light
- to receive the wrong amount of pay
- to sleep late
- a bank balance that is in the red

5   Work with some other students. Compare your company's culture with Microsoft's. First look at the photographs.

1 Do they surprise you in any way?
2 Could you wear trousers like Tony Ting's to work?
3 Do you have any facilities for employees' children?
4 How does your office compare with Doug Shepard's and Mark McPhee's?
5 Do you have any recreation areas like the courtyard?
6 How would your colleagues react if you took a pet snake to work?

6   Now describe and discuss what your company's culture is like. Consider

- hours of work and overtime
- over- or understaffing
- pay and expenses
- competitiveness
- how much responsibility is given at low levels of the organization
- the type of people who work there.

Famous for its *Windows* operating system, Microsoft is the world's No. 1 software company. With sales of over $3 billion, it's growing fast but the corporate culture remains strong. So, what's it like to work there?

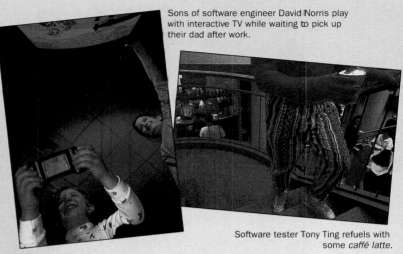

Sons of software engineer David Norris play with interactive TV while waiting to pick up their dad after work.

Software tester Tony Ting refuels with some *caffè latte*.

Hard work

Complaining about how hard you work at Microsoft is like complaining about the weather in Seattle. Everyone is overworked. Microsoft deliberately understaffs its product teams because it saves money, helps communication and encourages the fighting spirit.

Frugal

The pay may be good but there are no fancy expense accounts. Bill Gates, the CEO, is one of the richest men in America but he still flies economy class to Japan. Recently his administrative assistant was rushed off his feet by phone calls and letters and asked if he could hire someone to help out. "Who am I, the Queen?" asked Gates.

Competitive

Microsoft has been beaten in some markets by more sharply-focused competitors, but they keep fighting. They may get it wrong several times before they get it right but they never give up.

A rubber chicken hangs from art director Mark McPhee's desk.

The courtyard recreation area with software engineer Alistair Sutherland and his pet snake, Zsa Zsa.

Fun

Microsoft encourages individuality, and there are plenty of eccentric characters on the staff.

Product support engineer Doug Shepard answers users questions over the phone.

Tough

Microsoft employees are well-informed, logical and thick-skinned. They've got to be able to stand up for themselves when their bosses criticize them.

Challenging

Authority is pushed down through the ranks. Microsoft picks and chooses recruits from the graduates of the elite universities and business schools, then gives them lots of responsibility straight away.

OBJECTIVE

to discuss future work
plans and
arrangements

TASKS

to consider problems
that arise in
international meetings

•

to deal with
correspondence and
prioritize tasks

•

to exchange views on
environmental issues

•

to evaluate proposals
in a meeting and plan
how to implement
them

•

to write letters and
faxes making future
arrangements

PRESENTATION

1 🔲 Two managers are making preparations for a presentation.
Listen to their conversation. Look at the illustration and find the items
they mention.

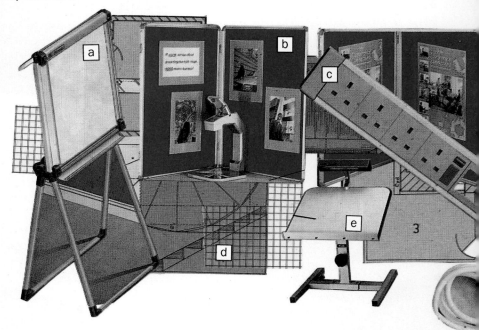

2 Who is going to do these things, Bob (B) or Victoire (V)?

1 give the presentation
2 hire a car
3 fax a map
4 use an overhead projector
5 take a projector to the office
6 bring a display stand
7 look through the briefing notes
8 meet someone for lunch

3 🔲 Complete the spaces in these extracts from the conversation.
Then listen again and check your answers.

Extract 1
Victoire I'm just phoning about your presentation next week. I think we
_____ check everything again.
Bob Again?
Victoire It's a big contract, Bob. I _____ think we
_____ take any chances.

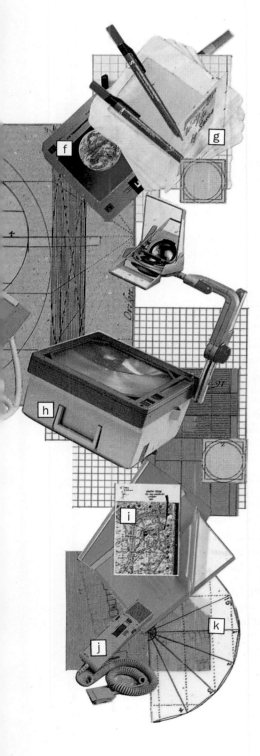

Extract 2

Bob I'm not sure where the office is.

Victoire _____ _____ _____ _____ take a taxi?

Bob No. I'm hiring a car.

Victoire Then _____ fax you a map with directions.

Bob Thanks.

Victoire Are you going to use an overhead projector?

Bob Yes.

Victoire Then we should take one with us.

Bob _____ I do that or _____ you?

Victoire _____ that to me.

4 Victoire and Bob had some disagreements. What were they about?

GRAMMAR NOTE

1 We can use _going to_ and _will_ to talk about future intentions. We use _will_ when we are making a decision at the moment of speaking.

A _I'm hiring a car._
B _Then I'll fax you a map with directions._ (I've just realized you will need one.)

We use _going to_ to talk about things we decided to do **before** the moment of speaking.
I'm going to bring some samples. (I've already decided.)
Are you going to use a projector? (What have you decided to do?)

2 We also use the present continuous tense to talk about future plans and arrangements.

I'm hiring a car.
Are you staying to watch my presentation?

So the present continuous and _going to_ have similar meanings.

I'm hiring a car. (I've made arrangements.)
I'm going to hire a car. (I've decided.)

---

5 What problems are you facing at work at the moment? Make a list of them. Tell a colleague how you intend to solve them. (Remember to use _'ll (will)_ when you are making instant decisions and _going to_ when you have already decided what to do.)

LANGUAGE WORK

International meetings ▌ You are attending a two-day conference at the international headquarters of your company. Top managers from all over the world are attending, but you encounter a few problems. Decide what to do about them, and tick one of the boxes.

---

1 **Before the conference, the organizers send you some working papers. You are short of time. Decide what to do with them.**

- ☐ I'll make sure I study the papers thoroughly, even if I have to stay up all night.
- ☐ I'll have a quick look at them on the plane.
- ☐ I'll do something else. (What?)

4 **The subject of this morning's meeting has little relevance to your area of work. You have a phone call to make and you'd like to leave half-way through. Decide what to do.**

- ☐ I'll leave without saying anything.
- ☐ I'll wait until the meeting is over to make my call.
- ☐ I'll do something else. (What?)

2 **Your Finance Director is supposed to attend the conference with you, but something important has come up and she can't. Decide what to do.**

- ☐ I'll go alone.
- ☐ I'll see if her deputy can attend instead, even though he has a much lower status in my organization.
- ☐ I'll do something else. (What?)

5 **The weather is very hot and the sun is beating through the meeting room windows. You are getting uncomfortable. Decide what to do.**

- ☐ I'll remove my jacket and loosen my tie.
- ☐ I'll do nothing.
- ☐ I'll do something else. (What?)

3 **This morning's meeting is supposed to be about next year's budget. However, you've had an idea about the distribution system that you'd prefer everyone to discuss. Decide what to do.**

- ☐ I'll keep quiet and discuss the budget.
- ☐ I'll introduce the topic of the distribution system.
- ☐ I'll do something else. (What?)

6 **You are sitting in a small meeting, listening to the Production Manager's report. You are not an expert on the subject of production but suddenly you have an idea. Decide what to do.**

- ☐ I'll indicate I'd like to speak and tell everyone my suggestion.
- ☐ I'll keep quiet and speak to the Production Manager later.
- ☐ I'll do something else. (What?)

7 **You are putting forward a proposal that several people at the meeting disagree with. You are absolutely sure that you are right and they are wrong. How will you handle this?**

- ☐ I'll stick to my guns.
- ☐ I'll drop the proposal.
- ☐ I'll do something else. (What?)

2 Tell a colleague what you've decided and explain why.

A *What are you going to do with the working papers?*
B *I think what's said at the meeting is more important than what's in the papers, so I'm going to look at them quickly.*
A *Are you? I'm not. I think ...*

3 Now compare your answers with these comments from John Mole. Does he mention your nationality at all? See if you agree with him.

John Mole *was educated at Oxford University and the international business school INSEAD. After a fifteen-year career with an American bank in the USA, the Middle East, and Europe, he became an independent writer and consultant on international human resources development.*

Preparing for international meetings

'Germans, Dutch and Danes will be well prepared. They will expect briefing papers which they will study and amend and whose implications they will have meticulously researched. British, Italian, Spanish, Irish and Greek participants will have skimmed through the papers on the plane and some may still be leafing through them at the meeting.'

Sending a subordinate

'If a participant cannot attend, British, Dutch and Danish managers will send a subordinate who may be much more junior. Spanish, French and North American managers will either send an immediate and trusted deputy or no one at all. Unaccustomed to meetings between people of different status, they will ignore the deputies of others.'

Sticking to the agenda

'Participants from the USA, Germany, Denmark and the Netherlands will expect to keep to the agenda. Participants from Portugal, Greece and Italy will feel free to introduce unscheduled topics at any time.'

Leaving a meeting

'Some participants, probably French or Italian, may feel less bound by the discipline of a meeting than others. They may leave to make phone calls or attend to paperwork if the discussion is not directly relevant to them. In the UK it is not acceptable to leave a meeting half-way through.'

Dress codes

'In most German offices, you keep your jacket on and buttoned up unless you are alone. Shirt sleeves are a sign of relaxation and not getting down to work. But in the Netherlands, taking off the jacket means getting down to work. In a Spanish meeting it is common to take off jackets and even loosen your tie.'

Contributing ideas

'At meetings in Germany, it is important to come very well prepared and not comment on things you are not qualified to speak about. In the Netherlands, everyone is expected to contribute, whatever their seniority.'

Dealing with conflict

'Commitment and tenacity, even to the point of obstinacy, are prized in the West. To change your mind, to abandon a position without a struggle, are signs of weakness. Sticking to your guns in an argument, not letting go, even in trivial matters, indicates strength of character. To a Japanese, it is the opposite.'

Glossary	
to amend	to change slightly
meticulously	very carefully
unaccustomed to	not used to
tenacity	being very determined and not giving up easily
obstinacy	stubbornness, refusing to change your mind or opinion
to abandon	to leave, to give up
a struggle	a fight
trivial	unimportant

Asking for opinions

1 Notice how *should* is used to ask for opinions in these questions.

Do you think | there should be higher | tax on cars?
| the government should increase |
| we should have higher |

| tax on cars should be increased?

2 Ask and answer the questions above.

Yes, I do | because ...
No, I don't |

Yes, I think | there | should. What do you think?
| they |
| we |

Solar power station, Font Romeu, France

3 Work with a partner. Find out where they stand on some green issues. Structure your questions in different ways. Use these ideas.

1   subsidize public transport
2   no tax on unleaded petrol
3   more recycling plants
4   less packaging on consumer goods
5   build more nuclear power stations
6   only invest in renewable forms of energy
7   heavier fines for companies who pollute the environment
8   all cycle to work

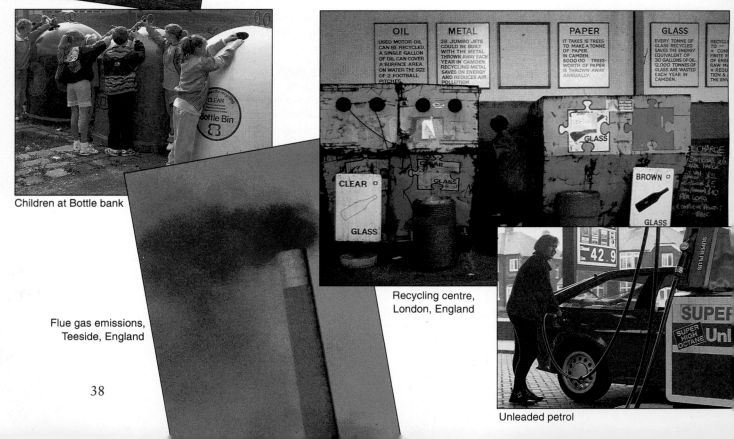

Children at Bottle bank

Flue gas emissions, Teeside, England

Recycling centre, London, England

Unleaded petrol

Managing the environment

You are concerned about the environment and increasing levels of pollution. As directors of a small manufacturing company, you have decided it is time to act, no matter how small your contributions may be.

1 Work in small groups. You have introduced a company suggestion scheme and collected the proposals below from your staff. Hold a meeting to decide what to do with each of their ideas.

You can

- dismiss them
- implement them immediately
- investigate the ideas further.

If you decide to implement a proposal, or investigate it further, plan what to do. Decide who will be responsible and what resources they will need.

Useful phrases

I'll do that, if you like.   *I'll leave that to you.*
Shall I do that or will you?   *I'll need …*

Suggestion scheme proposals

1 Take away all company cars. Provide bicycles instead and bus or train tickets.

2 Scrap the company's fleet of lorries. Replace them with new models that are more economical on fuel.

3 Encourage staff to work at home. Telecommunications can substitute for travel.

4 Instead of working five eight-hour days each week, work four ten-hour days. A three-day weekend will reduce the factory's heating costs.

5 Change all the conventional light bulbs in the building to compact fluorescent light bulbs, which use 20% of the power and last longer.

6 Install solar cells in the roof to collect sunlight to heat the offices.

7 Put less packaging on our products.

8 Tell our suppliers to provide less packaging with their products.

9 Plant trees in the garden to stabilize the soil, conserve water resources and 'fix' carbon dioxide to help slow the pace of global warming.

10 Ban all office memos to save paper.

11 Collect all waste paper from offices at the end of each day and send it for recycling.

12 Only sell vegetarian food in the canteen.

13 Make a contribution from the company's profits to the Green Party or green pressure groups.

14 Stop trying to make the company expand. Make economic efficiency our goal instead of economic growth.

15 Install a large fan on the hillside outside the factory to blow away pollution.

2 You would like to award a prize to the staff member who submitted the best suggestion. Decide which one you think is best and what the prize should be.

3 Now compare your decisions with your colleagues from other groups. Find out which proposals they decided to implement and why.

Pronunciation   **1**    Listen and repeat this sentence.

I think we should implement this proposal immediately.

Notice the /ɪ/ sounds.
I think we should implement this proposal immediately.

And notice the /iː/ sounds.
I think we should implement this proposal immediately.

Can you hear the difference between these two sounds?

2   What sounds do these words contain: is it /ɪ/ or /iː/?

least	fill	slip	leave
list	feel	sleep	live

Listen to the words and repeat them.

3   Read the sentences and replies below, then listen to the tape. You will hear the sentences in a different order. Make the appropriate reply after each one.

1 Who's got the <u>least</u>?   I haven't got many.
2 Who's got the <u>list</u>?   Me. What do you want to know?

3 I can't <u>feel</u> it.   Take your gloves off, then.
4 I can't <u>fill</u> it.   You need to turn the tap on.

5 I don't want to <u>sleep</u>.   Yes, it's difficult if you've got jet lag.
6 I don't want to <u>slip</u>.   Yes. It's very icy.

7 Where does he <u>leave</u>?   From Platform 9.
8 Where does he <u>live</u>?   In Istanbul.

4   Practise the sentences with a partner. One person should read a sentence. The other should listen carefully and decide which reply to make.

SKILLS WORK

Speaking

Team work

1 Work with a partner. It's Monday 12th February and you both work for the Sales department of Alert Systems, a security alarm manufacturer. Your boss, Claire Patterson, is away visiting the States for a few days so you are covering for her. Look at the papers in her in-tray on pages 42–43.

1 Decide which problems are urgent and which ones can wait.
2 Decide what you will do about the urgent problems. (Which one of you will do it?)

2 Change partners and compare notes with another student. Tell them what you decided and find out what they're going to do.

Writing

Look at the different documents on pages 42–43.

1 Find the letters and faxes. What differences in layout and style do you notice? Consider

- the positions of the address and date
- the opening greetings
- the endings

For more information on the layout of letters and faxes, see page 187 of the Grammar and Usage notes.

2 What do these abbreviations mean?

| encs | TNKS | pp | PLS | Re | Dept. |
| cc | incl. | RGDS | ATTN | asap | PDQ |

Would you expect to read them in a letter, a fax, or a telex?

3 We use a lot of standard phrases in letters and faxes. Find standard phrases in the examples on pages 42–43 that are used to
- refer to another letter, fax, or call
- give good news
- give bad news
- offer help
- make requests
- apologize
- refer to future contact.

Scott Management Training
A COMMITMENT TO EXCELLENCE

Scott Management Training
Tudor House
Redbridge Road
Wicken
Wolverton
Bucks

Tel: 0908 571286
Fax: 0908 571326

5 February 19--

Marketing Director
Alert Systems Ltd
Cowpepper Road
Jericho
Oxford OX2 6DP

Dear Sir or Madam,

As a sales executive in today's business climate, you will be well aware of the need to deliver rapid results. I am delighted to tell you that Scott Management Training will be running a one-day seminar in Oxford on 15 March which will enable you to do just that.

So that you can find out more about the concrete benefits of an SMT sales seminar, I am enclosing a demonstration cassette tape along with details of the day's programme and priority booking forms. To ensure participants receive personal attention, we are limiting places at the seminar to 25. As we expect demand to be high, we advise early booking.

If we can be of further assistance, please do not hesitate to contact our Customer Service Department.

Yours faithfully,

Barbara Sanders

pp Jacky Scott
<u>Managing Director</u>

encs:

Scott Management plc Directors: Jacky Scott, Simon Barnes, Richard Baldwin, Anne Broadhead. Registered Office: Cedar House, Pound Close, Wicken, Wolverton, Bucks. Telephone: 01908 57286 Telefax: 01908 57326 Registered in England No 18753628903.

Gold Shield Security

TELEFAX TRANSMISSION

HEAD OFFICE:
171-173 Hartlington Court
Long Wall
London EC4 RS5

Telephone: 071 837 529
Fax: 071 837 826

To:	Claire Patterson, Sales Director, Alert Systems Ltd	Date:	9 February
From:	Alan Wilson, MD	Pages:	1
Re:	My visit to Oxford		

Further to our meeting last month, you will be pleased to hear that Dr Piti Hutasingh is interested in acting as your agent in Thailand, He is visiting London next week. If you wish, I would be happy to bring him with me when I come to see you in Oxford next Thursday.

Could you possibly arrange accommodation for us for one night at the Randolph Hotel?

Looking forward to seeing you on the 15th.

ASW

The new brochures have come back from the printers. Would you like me to send them to the sales offices or do you want to check them first?

They have sent the invoice too, but they seem to have undercharged us by £600. What shall I do?

Peter

42

TELEPHONE MESSAGE

To: CLAIRE PATTERSON (SALES DEPT)

in your absence

MR / (MRS) MISS   ISAACS

of   THE EXPRESS

Telephone No: 0799 267698

and left the following message

SHE'S A REPORTER FROM THE EXPRESS AND SHE'S RUNG THREE TIMES. SAYS IT CAN'T WAIT. SOMETHING ABOUT AN ALARM SYSTEM WE SOLD THAT DIDN'T WORK. PLS. PHONE HER BACK.

Signed: Charles

Date: Monday 12th Feb   Time: 10.30am

TELEX

TO: THE SALES TEAM

CHANGE OF PLAN. NOW CATCHING FLIGHT BACK ON FRIDAY 16TH - NOT WEDNESDAY 14TH. ARRIVING 18.10, BA 002 FROM NEW YORK. PLS PICK ME UP FROM HEATHROW TERMINAL 4.

SEE YOU SOON

TNKS

CLAIRE

Construcciones Escobar

Construcciones Escobar
Calle de los Alamos 42044
Concepción
Chile

Tfno. 2234698
Telefax. 24181361

5 February 19--

Re: Our order ref. 7256-89

Dear Claire,

Thank you for your letter of 18 January enquiring about our shipment requirements for the above order. I am sorry about the delay in replying but I have been away for a few days.

As you know, we planned to install the alarm system in a new government building that was under construction. Unfortunately we have just heard that all building work has been stopped until further notice so I'm afraid we must cancel the order.

I am sorry for any inconvenience caused but I'm sure you realise that it is due to circumstances beyond our control. I will of course contact you again if building work is resumed.

Yours sincerely,

Hugo

Hugo Garrido Escobar
Director

Cherwell Catering

fax

Attention of: David Ellingham (Finance Dept)	From: Colin Scott (Outside Contracts)
No. Pages incl. top sheet 1	Time/Date: 09.30am 9th February

Please telephone us immediately if you do not receive the number of pages indicated

Dear David,

Re: Lunch arrangements

With reference to our phone conversation yesterday, I am writing to confirm that we can provide lunch for nine people in your executive suite at 1 p.m. on Friday 24 February.

Here are two alternative menus. We would be grateful if you could let us know which you would prefer by 16 February.

Menu 1

Melon and Parma ham
Spicy fried chicken
Chocolate gâteau

Menu 2

Onion soup
Roast pork and apple sauce
Crème caramel

If you have any further questions, please do not hesitate to ask.

Best regards

Colin Scott
Colin Scott

CHERWELL CATERING
HOLBART WAY
OXFORD
OXFORDSHIRE OX3 8NP
TEL: 0865 267683 FAX: 0865 267622

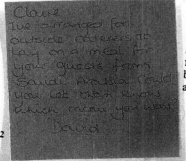

Claire
I've arranged for
outside caterers to
lay on a meal for
your guests from
Saudi Arabia. Could
you let them know
which menu you want?

David

Alert Systems Ltd

PRIVATE & CONFIDENTIAL

MEMORANDUM

To:	Claire Patterson	From:	Andrew Tiffany
c.c.	Carlo Baldi (Marketing)	Date:	12 February 19--
Re:	Budget Cuts		

** ** **

I regret to inform you that we must look for further reductions in our spending on sales promotions and advertising. I'm calling an urgent meeting for tomorrow (Tuesday) at 9.00a.m. in my office to discuss next month's budget. I realize this is very short notice, but I'd appreciate it if you could attend.

A.T.

43

4 Make yourself a checklist of useful phrases for future reference. Complete the table below with words and phrases from the box.

Would you like me to ...?	I am afraid ...	please do not hesitate to ask.
You will be pleased to hear that ...	Please find enclosed ...	Further to ...
enquire ...	seeing you on the 29th.	Could you possibly ...?
	any inconvenience caused.	

Starting	We are writing to	advise you of ...
		confirm ...

Stating a reference	Thank you for your letter of January 23.	
	With reference to	our telephone conversation today, ...
	------------------------------------	your fax of June 5th, ...
Giving good news	I am delighted to tell you that...	

Giving bad news	We regret to inform you that ...	
	Unfortunately ...	

Making a request	We would be grateful if you could ...	
	I would appreciate it if you could ...	

	Please ...	
Offering help	If you wish, we would be happy to ...	

Apologizing	I am sorry about the delay in replying.	
	I would like to apologize for ...	
	We are sorry for ------------------------------------	
Enclosing documents	I am enclosing ...	

Closing remarks	If you have any further questions, ------------------------------------	
	If we can help in any way, please contact us again.	
	Thank you for your help.	
Referring to future contact	I look forward to	meeting you next week.
	Looking forward to	receiving your comments in due course.
		------------------------------------

5 *We regret to inform you that* ... is more formal than *I am afraid* ...
Can you find more examples of formal and informal language in the
table?

6 A fax is quicker and more urgent than a letter, but a letter is more
formal and confidential. What would you send in the following situations:
a letter or a fax? How would you begin and finish it? Write the opening
and closing phrases.

1 You have heard that Ms Parker, a colleague from your London office,
   will be visiting your company next month. You need to offer to book
   a hotel for her.
2 You'd like a colleague who works at your organization's subsidiary in
   Melbourne to send you copies of all Australian press cuttings that
   refer to your company.
3 Your copy of *Newsweek* hasn't been arriving recently. Perhaps your
   subscription has run out. You'd like to find out.
4 Mr Kulesza from Poland phoned you this morning to ask for a
   demonstration of one of your products. You need to tell him you've
   spoken to someone in your Warsaw sales office and that they will be
   in contact shortly to make arrangements.
5 Mr Liu wrote and asked you to speak at a conference in Taiwan.
   Unfortunately you can't go.
6 Signor Masera phoned and asked for directions to your office from the
   airport. You promised to send him a map.
7 You met Frau Gräber at a meeting in Geneva several weeks ago and
   promised to send her a copy of an article you read on time
   management. You have only just got round to sending it.

7 Now try writing one of the letters or faxes out in full. Refer to pages
186-187 of the Grammar and Usage notes for information on layout.

TASKS

to follow an account of the growth of a market
•
to read a career history
•
to exchange information about work experiences
•
to give an account of a business problem
•
to discuss turning points in a company's history

PRESENTATION

A spreadsheet programme

Trying out a programme

1   Do you have a PC (personal computer)? What sort of software packages do you use? Where did you buy them?

2   [▭]   Fifty per cent of all the PC software sold in Japan is distributed through SOFTBANK. Listen to a SOFTBANK manager talking about the growth and development of his company and answer these questions.

1   He mentions three product areas that have shown strong growth. Number them in the order they took off.

☐   Business applications
☐   Networking
☐   Games

A range of business software

14 computer magazines

Using the mouse

Consulting the catalogue

2 He talks about the development of the computer magazine business. Number these events in the order they happened.

- [ ] They decided to take a gamble.
- [ ] The magazines didn't sell.
- [ ] The magazines sold out in three days.
- [ ] They set up the publishing division.
- [ ] They set up the distribution business.
- [ ] They changed the layout of the magazines.
- [ ] They launched two magazines.
- [ ] They advertised the magazines on TV.

3 🔲 Listen again and answer these questions.

1 How long has SOFTBANK been in business?
2 What networking products does he mention?
3 How many computer magazines did they publish last month?
4 When did they set up the publishing division?
5 Why didn't they close it down when it wasn't successful?

4 Complete these sentences about SOFTBANK. Fill each space with the correct form of the verb *distribute*. Think carefully about what tense to use.

1 SOFTBANK _____ software since 1981.
2 When the business first started, no other companies _____ software in Japan.
3 After they _____ software for six months, they set up a publishing division.
4 Last year they _____ over 50% of the PC software sold in Japan.

47

LANGUAGE WORK

A career

1 Work with some colleagues. Read the true story about the career of a young émigré on the opposite page. Pause at each question and guess what he did next. Say which alternative you think is most likely.

2 Number these events in Jan Ludwig Hoch's life in the right order.

☐ He lost control of Pergamon Press.
☐ He took the company public.
☐ He served in the British army.
☐ He launched a weekly newspaper called *The European*.
☐ He ran an import company that later became Pergamon Press.
☐ He regained control of Pergamon Press.
☑ He avoided persecution by fleeing Czechoslovakia.
☐ He was involved in a scandal.
☐ He changed his identity.

3 Study the verbs in the sentences above. Notice the words they are used with. What other words could they be used with?
For example, as well as losing control we can also *lose money, lose an argument, lose a client* and *lose contact with someone.*

4 Match each verb with one of the groups of words.

1	take	**a**	a new product, a satellite, an attack, a career
2	serve	**b**	a person you don't like, accidents, mistakes, the vehicle in front
3	launch		
4	run	**c**	a break, care, a shower, a photograph
5	regain	**d**	money, your mind, suppliers, direction
6	avoid	**e**	around, an experiment, late, a risk, for president
7	be involved in	**f**	dinner, a customer, a purpose, someone right
8	change	**g**	your work, a fight, politics, decision-making
		h	your freedom, power, your health, market share

Finding things in common

When you meet new business acquaintances, it's always nice to find out whether you have things in common. Ask a colleague questions about their life and business career. Find out about
- where they were born
- what their parents did
- the schools they attended
- the qualifications they got
- their first job
- jobs they had after that.

Try to establish some experiences you have both shared.
We both studied history at university.
Neither of us was very good at mathematics when we were at school.

WHO WAS JAN LUDWIG HOCH?

1 In 1938, fifteen-year old Jan Ludwig Hoch fled Czechoslovakia to avoid Nazi persecution. He changed his identity and what do you think he did next?

a Went to Russia and fought with the Red army.
b Stayed in Europe and fought with the French Resistance.
c Got a ticket on a boat going to the US by working as a cook.

Turn to 4 to find out.

2 What are you doing reading this? Shouldn't you be looking at number 4?

3 He lost his seat in parliament after he was involved in a scandal. Saul Steinberg, a New York financier, pulled out of a deal to buy Pergamon and claimed he had lied about how much the company was worth. As well as losing his parliamentary seat, he also lost control of Pergamon. The Board of Directors ousted him and the British authorities said he was unfit to run a public company. What do you think he did next?

a Regained control of Pergamon Press.
b Bought a German publishing company.
c Acquired a stake in a TV station in Australia.

Turn to 6 to find out.

4 In fact, he fought for the French Resistance, and after the fall of France, served in the British army with distinction. What do you think he did at the end of the war?

a Returned to Czechoslovakia and set up a shipping company.
b Studied International Law at the Sorbonne in Paris.
c Ran an import company from the UK.

Turn to 7 to find out.

5 In fact, he was elected to the British parliament for the Labour Party. What do you think he did next?

a Became Prime Minister.
b Became a cabinet minister for the Department of Trade and Industry.
c Lost his seat in parliament.

Turn to 3 to find out.

6 He regained control of Pergamon, then he entered the newspaper business, buying *The Mirror Group*, publishers of one of the UK's largest national daily papers. What do you think he did next?

a Bought *Berlitz* (language instruction materials publishers).
b Bought *Colliers* (encyclopaedia publishers).
c Bought *Que* (computer manuals publishers).

Turn to 8 to find out.

7 In fact, he imported scientific journals from Germany for a London based joint venture company. He later bought the company, named it *Pergamon Press* and *took it public. What do you think he did next?

a Took a stake in a Japanese radio station.
b Got elected to the British parliament.
c Set up an airline company.

Turn to 5 to find out.

8 In fact, he bought all three companies and several more besides. Then he went on to launch a weekly pan-European newspaper, *The European*. What do you think he did next?

a Retired and moved back to Czechoslovakia.
b Received the Queen's Award for industry.
c Fell off the side of his yacht into the Atlantic.

Turn to File 12, page 156 to find out.

* Its shares became listed on the Stock Exchange.

Past experiences   **1**   Masayoshi Son was born in Kyushu, Japan in 1957. He is the founder of SOFTBANK, Japan's leading PC software distributor. Read his account of how he came to start the business and work out how long it took him to decide what to do.

I spent a long time doing research and making business plans before I started the company. I was living in Kyushu at the time. It was 1979 and I'd just come back from the States. I had no income and all my family and friends were worried. They couldn't understand why I wasn't doing anything, but I was thinking.

I'd gone to the States to study when I was sixteen. I went to Oakland, California for a couple of years first, then transferred to Berkeley where I graduated. I met my wife while I was studying English in Oakland and by the time we came back to Kyushu we had a new baby. She was worried too. I had come up with 40 new business ideas – everything from creating software to setting up hospital chains – but I didn't know which to start.

I wanted a business I could fall in love with. It had to be unique and original. It had to have great growth potential. I had about 25 points like this and I took a big sheet of paper and gave each business idea scores. Then I picked the best one. It turned out to be the personal computer software business. So in 1981 we finally moved to Tokyo and I started SOFTBANK.

2   Complete this time line. Write the dates Masayoshi Son moved from one place to another above and the places he has lived underneath.

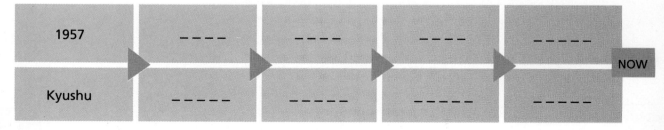

GRAMMAR NOTE

Study these sentences.
He lived in the States for six years.
He's lived / been living in Tokyo since 1981.

1 In these sentences we use the past tense for actions that are finished and the present perfect tense for actions that are still continuing now.

2 We use *for* to talk about periods of time and *since* to talk about points in time.

3 Both these sentences are correct
He's been living in Tokyo since 1981.
He's lived in Tokyo since 1981.

In this situation, they mean virtually the same thing, but we tend to use the continuous form if it's possible. Sometimes it isn't — for example with verbs like *be* and *have*.
How long has he been in Tokyo?
NOT *How long has he been being in Tokyo?*
How long has he had his own business?
NOT *How long has he been having his own business?*

3 Work with a partner. Ask and answer questions about Masayoshi Son's career. Begin each question with *How long ...?*
A *How long did he stay in Oakland?*
B *(He stayed there) for two years.*
A *And how long has he been living in Tokyo?*

1 stay in Oakland
2 live in Tokyo
3 be unemployed
4 run a software distribution company
5 study at Berkeley
6 spend deciding what business to start
7 have his own business

4 Now ask your partner similar questions about themselves.

1 What company do you work for?
2 How long have you worked there?
3 What job did you have before this one?
4 How long were you there?
5 Where do you live?
6 How long have you lived there?
7 When did you move there?

Traveller's stories

I Read the beginnings of these true travellers' stories and match them to the right endings.

1

Sir Colin Marshall, Chief Executive of British Airways, was having difficulty finding his way in New York. A woman was passing by so he stopped her and asked for directions. The woman pulled down her dark glasses and stared at him angrily.

2

Tom Brown's Skoda had broken down so he had left it on the motorway and returned home by train. But 73-year-old Tom felt worried. He was sure he had forgotten something. What had he left behind? Half way through tea he remembered.

3

A fisherman was working in a Norwegian fjord one day when he found a boat with nobody in it. Thinking it was adrift, he tied it to his own boat and towed it ashore. This did not please the scuba diver who popped up out of the water and found his boat had gone.

4

A journalist from *The Times* newspaper was watching his suitcase vanish into the X-ray machine at Tangier airport when he suddenly remembered he had packed two antique guns inside. Terrified, he rushed to the operator and explained what he had done.

A

He had left Mrs Brown sitting on the back seat.

B

It took him four hours to swim home.

C

"Do I look like a goddam road map?" she asked.

D

"Don't worry sir," came the reply. "Our machines will never pick them up."

---

2 Look at the first story again. Two past tenses are used to tell this story. What tense is used to
1 set the scene and describe the circumstances of the story?
2 describe the main events in the story?

3 Look at the second story again. Two past tenses are used to tell this story too. What tense is used to describe
1 events that happened after Tom returned home?
2 events that happened before he returned home?

4 Look at the third and fourth stories again. Underline all the examples of the past continuous and past perfect tense. Explain why these tenses are used.

For more information on when we use the past simple, continuous and perfect tenses, see pages 174-175 in the Grammar and Usage notes.

5 Now tell a short story about something that happened to you when you were travelling. For example; losing your way, being checked by security, a car breakdown.

SKILLS WORK

Speaking
Managing change
Think of an important event that took place in your work place in the past. It should be an event that resulted in a change in your way of working. It could be
- the introduction of a new system
- an improvement you made to a process
- a technical development
- the purchase of new equipment.

Tell a colleague about it.

1 Describe the background to the event. Say what you were doing before and what the previous system had been.
2 Explain the change you made.
3 Describe what happened as a result of the change.

Listening
1 What do you know about the LEGO toy manufacturing company?

53

2 🔲 Listen to eight short extracts from a talk about the early history of the LEGO company. Stop the tape after each one and match the extract with an event on the graph.

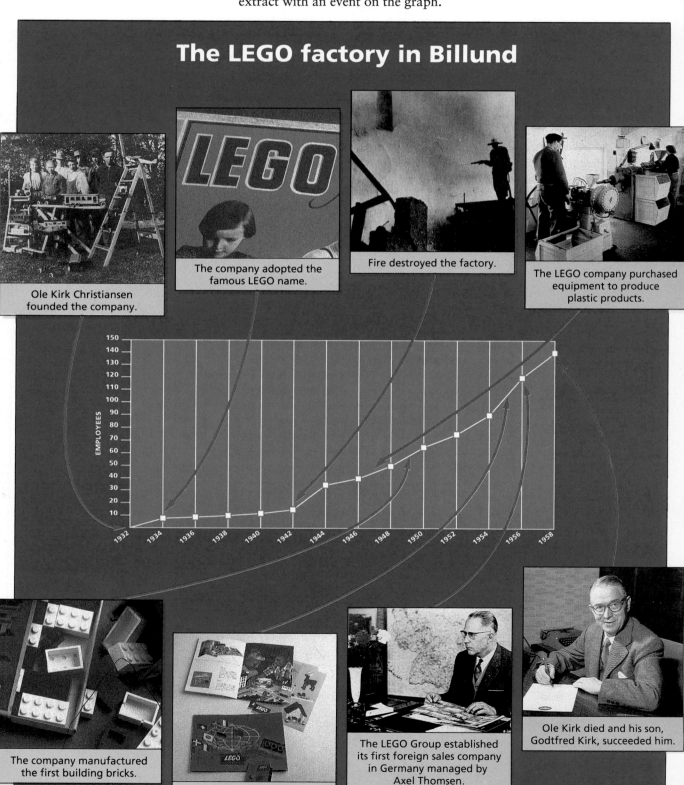

The LEGO factory in Billund

Ole Kirk Christiansen founded the company.

The company adopted the famous LEGO name.

Fire destroyed the factory.

The LEGO company purchased equipment to produce plastic products.

The company manufactured the first building bricks.

The company launched their system of play.

The LEGO Group established its first foreign sales company in Germany managed by Axel Thomsen.

Ole Kirk died and his son, Godtfred Kirk, succeeded him.

(Graph: EMPLOYEES, axis 10–150, years 1932–1958)

3 🔲 Listen again and answer these questions.

1 What sales terms did LEGO offer retailers on their original building bricks?
2 When Ole Kirk founded the company, what did it produce?
3 How old was Godtfred when he started working for the company?
4 What potential did Godtfred see in the building bricks?
5 Why was the factory fire such a disaster?
6 Who was Axel Thomsen?
7 Where did the name LEGO come from?
8 What did the Danish toy trade magazine say about plastics?

4 Do you know anything about the history of your company? Has it always sold the same products/services as it does now? How have its markets changed over time? What events have been significant turning points?

5 Think about your work experiences. What was
- the best idea you've ever had?
- your biggest stroke of luck?
- the greatest coincidence you've ever experienced?
- your saddest moment?
- your happiest moment?
- the best piece of advice you've ever received?
- the worst piece of advice you've ever received?

Tell your colleagues about some of these experiences.

Pronunciation Regular verbs ending in -ed are pronounced in three ways /d/, /t/, and /ɪd/.

/d/ *discovered, realized*
/t/ *looked, produced*
/ɪd/ *suggested, depended*

🔲 Listen to the sentences from the graph. Which sound does each verb end in? Tick the correct column.

	/d/	/t/	/ɪd/
founded adopted destroyed purchased manufactured launched established died succeeded			

55

OBJECTIVE

to explore possible
solutions to business
problems

TASKS

to make, accept, and
reject suggestions

•

to consider the
possible outcomes of
different courses of
action

•

to evaluate proposals
for dealing with a
security problem

•

to negotiate solutions
in conflict situations

•

to follow accounts of
business problems and
suggest solutions

PRESENTATION

I   Look at the pictures. What problems do you think the people are
discussing?

2   ▭   Now listen to some managers discussing some problems. What
problems are they trying to solve? Match each conversation with the right
picture.

3 🔲 Now listen again. Fill the spaces in these sentences.

Conversation 1

_____ _____ _____ the Metro?

_____ _____ _____ _____ a taxi?

Conversation 2

Have they _____ _____ yet?

_____ _____ phone them up and explain what's happened.

Conversation 3

We _____ try.

That might be _____ _____ . How much do they

_____ for a call out?

Conversation 4

_____ _____ _____ _____ put everyone

on overtime.

No, it's _____ _____ _____ .

Conversation 5

If _____ _____ thirty, what discount _____

_____ _____ _____ ?

What if _____ _____ a hundred?

4 In Exercise 2 you heard all these words to do with making payments.

salary	wages	charge	fees	fare	commission	tip

Which one describes the money you pay

1 to thank someone for their services (for example, a waiter or waitress)?
2 to an agent or salesperson?
3 for a service (for example, electricity, postage)?
4 for a professional service (for example, to a lawyer)?
5 for travelling?
6 to your staff every week?
7 to your staff every month?

5 Now use the same seven words to complete these sentences.

1 The taxi _____ was $18 and I gave the driver a $4 _____ .
2 On orders of over 2,000 pieces delivery is free of _____ .
3 The builders receive their weekly _____ in cash.
4 In addition to your basic _____ you will receive a 25% _____ on all goods sold.
5 She's a good accountant but her _____ are high.

LANGUAGE WORK

Making suggestions

1 These phrases are often used to make suggestions

I think we should ...
How about ..?
We could ...
We'd better ...
Why don't we ...?

Which phrases are most and least forceful?
Which phrase is followed by a gerund (an *-ing* form)?
What does *'d* stand for in *We'd better ...*?
What are the negative forms of *I think we should ...* and *We'd better*?

2 The following phrases can all be used to respond to other people's suggestions. Grade them according to how positive they sound. Give 1 to the most enthusiastic and 5 to the most negative.

I don't think we should.
That's a good idea.
I'm not sure about that.
No, that's simply not feasible.
That might be the answer.

3 Work with a partner. Discuss different ways of tackling these problems. Don't forget to respond to one another's suggestions.

1 You manufacture skis, so demand for your products is seasonal. You'd like to make another product, something that sells in the summer, but what?

2 You have organized a two-day seminar for 160 people on quality management. It's due to start in an hour and your famous guest speaker has lost her voice.

3 You print a monthly bulletin for the staff. It contains general news about your company but it looks boring so nobody reads it. How can you make it more interesting?

4 Someone has been hacking into confidential files on your computer system.

5 You produce toothpaste and mouthwashes. You want to persuade your customers, the retailers, to give more shelf space to your products.

6 Your company's sales manager disappeared while on a business trip to Sicily last week. Her husband and two children have been frantic with worry. A letter has arrived saying that, if you want to see her alive again, you must pay $200,000 and you mustn't speak to the police.

Considering possibilities

1   Read this conversation with a partner.

A *We'd like to order 500. What discount will you give us?*
B *If you order 500, we'll give you 10%.*
A *What if we ordered more?*
B *If you ordered 5,000, we'd give you a 15% discount.*

Look at B's replies.

1 What words do the contractions *'ll* and *'d* represent?
2 Both B's replies are about future possibilities. But what tenses do they contain?
3 How do B's replies differ in meaning?

2   Look at the list of possible future events and decide how probable they are. Are they

1 things which might happen?
2 things which could happen in theory but probably won't happen in practice?

a A head-hunter offers you another job.
b You get promoted.
c Your company makes you redundant.
d You decide to start your own business.
e The president of your country invites you to dinner.
f You finish work early tomorrow.
g You become chairman of the company you work for.
h Your English teacher gives you a lot of homework.
i You learn to speak perfect English.
j You get stuck in a *lift.
k You buy a new car next year.
l Someone offers you a job in another country.
m Your bank balance goes into the red.
n You win a million dollars.

*US English: *elevator*

3   Now make sentences about these possible events. If you think something might happen, use a first conditional form.

If a head-hunter offers me another job, I'll accept if the salary is higher.

If you think something is unlikely to happen, use a second conditional form.

If I got promoted, I'd be delighted.

For more information on these conditional forms, see page 180 of the Grammar and Usage notes.

Pronunciation

1 🔲 Listen to these short conversations about possible future events. Decide how probable B thinks each event is. Does B say *'ll (will)* or *'d (would)*? Put the verbs in brackets into the correct tense.

1 A That head-hunter phoned for you again today.
  B Don't worry. If he (offer) me a job, I (refuse).

2 A Another building firm's gone bankrupt.
  B If the recession (continue), we (all be) out of business.

3 A They're thinking of relocating their headquarters.
  B If they (move) up north, it (be) easier to attract staff.

4 A Don't miss your flight, whatever you do.
  B I know. If I (arrive) late, they (be) furious.

5 A We need to keep our prices as low as possible.
  B If energy costs (increase), we (have to) raise them.

6 A They're planning to make more job cuts.
  B If they (make) me redundant, I (start) my own business.

2 *-ll* and *-d* are very short sounds but it is still important to say them. Practise reading the conversations with a partner.

A shrinkage problem

1 You run a chain of small newsagent's shops. You have an increasing number of problems with 'shrinkage' — that is, loss of stock through theft. You suspect members of staff are as much to blame as the public.

On the opposite page are some proposals for dealing with the problem. Go through them one by one and consider what will or would happen if you implemented them.

Proposal 1 is a good idea. If we position tills at the exits, it'll make it more difficult to steal.
I don't like proposal 2. The staff would object if we issued uniforms with no pockets.

2 Do you have any other suggestions for dealing with this shrinkage problem?

3 Work in small groups. Hold a meeting. Discuss the proposals and decide which ones to implement.

SUGGESTIONS FOR DEALING WITH 'SHRINKAGE'

1. Position tills in front of the exits.

2. Issue staff with uniforms with no pockets.

3. Run courses training staff to look out for thieves.

4. Put electronic tags or labels on products to trigger alarms at exits.

5. Pay staff well so they don't need to steal.

6. Give staff larger discounts so they feel less tempted to steal.

7. Install more mirrors in the shops.

8. Keep more detailed stock figures.

9. Put clauses in staff's employment contracts permitting searches of their belongings.

10. Employ more staff so they have more time to observe customers (and each other).

VOCABULARY NOTE

Do you know when to use the verbs *to control* and *to check*?

To control means to manage or regulate something.
It was a difficult meeting for the chairperson to control.
This knob controls the radio's volume.

To check means to examine something to make sure it is correct.
Count the boxes on the shelf and check none have been stolen.
Check the bill and make sure they haven't overcharged us.

But *to check* can also mean to make something go more slowly or to hold it back.
The government is trying to check public expenditure.

In this sense, it is similar to *control*.

4 Have you ever had problems with theft in your work place? How did you deal with them? Were the thieves caught and, if so, how?

Negotiating solutions

1 Read this conversation with a partner. Notice the customer's questions. They use conditional forms to suggest compromises.

Customer   *If we order 1,000, will you include free delivery?*
Supplier   *Yes, we could agree to that.*
Customer   *And if we paid in advance, would you increase our discount?*
Supplier   *I'm afraid that wouldn't be possible.*

Work with a partner. Make up similar conversations using these ideas.

1   **Customer and supplier**
    order today, deliver by Friday?
    pay in advance, reduce the price by 2%?

2   **Landlord and tenant**
    employ more security staff, sign a 5-year lease?
    lower the rent, pay for building repairs?

3   **Sales representatives and management**
    accept higher sales targets, increase our commission?
    not reach our targets, still pay our bonus?

4   **Bank and client**
    pay a higher rate of interest, give us the loan?
    not offer our home as security, still lend us the money?

2 Here are some business problems where a solution needs to be negotiated. Act them out with a partner. Take different sides and try to negotiate an agreement. Perhaps you can find a compromise solution.

1   Every Christmas a company gives its customers gifts ranging from diaries and calendars to cases of scotch whisky. The financial manager says it's too expensive and wants to stop. The sales manager disagrees.

2   The management of a company wants its staff to refuse all gifts from suppliers, no matter how small they may be. They are worried that the buyers will be put in compromising positions. The buyers say this would not happen and feel the management is being unreasonable.

3   A manager feels overworked and in need of more help, particularly in busy periods. They want to take on a full-time assistant. Their boss, however, is under pressure to reduce costs and is unwilling to agree.

4   The management of a company wants to make its security staff redundant and contract the work out to an independent operator. It would save money but the unions don't like it.

5   A large automotive company wants one of its small suppliers to make deliveries daily and with only two hours' notice. The supplier says this means they will have to carry much larger stocks, which they can't afford to do.

Payment

> ☆ **pay¹** /peɪ/ *noun* [U] money that you get regularly for work that you have done: *It's a dirty job but the pay is good.* ○ *a pay increase* ☛ **Pay** is the general word for money that you get regularly for work that you have done. **Wages** are paid weekly or daily in cash. A **salary** is paid monthly, directly into a bank account. You pay a **fee** for professional services, eg to a doctor, lawyer, etc. **Payment** is money that you get for work that you do once or not regularly.
>
> ☆ **pay²** /peɪ/ *verb* (*pt, pp* **paid**) **1** [I,T] **pay (sb) (for sth)**; **pay sth (to sb) (for sth)** to give sb money for sth: *She is very well paid.* ○ *Do you want to pay by cheque or by credit card?* ○ *The work's finished but we haven't paid the builders yet.* ○ *to be paid by the hour* ○ *We paid the dealer £3 000 for the car.* **2** [T] **pay sth (to sb)** to give the money that you owe for sth: *Have you paid the gas bill?* **3** [I,T] to make a profit; to be worth doing: *The factory closed down because the owners couldn't make it pay.* ○ *It would pay you to get professional advice before making a decision.*

Extract from *The Oxford Wordpower Dictionary*, 1993

1 Study this dictionary entry for the word *pay*. How many different meanings can you find?

2 What do these signs and symbols mean?

/peɪ/   *noun* (U)   ☛

verb (*pt, pp* **paid**)   (I,T)   pay (sb) (for sth)

3 Here are some sentences containing the word *pay*. Some of them contain mistakes. Find the ones that are wrong and correct them. Look back at the example sentences in the dictionary entry if you're not sure.

1 Pay is generally higher in the north than in the south.
2 He's badly paid.
3 Can I pay in credit card?
4 Have you paid the waiter yet?
5 Have you paid the meal yet?
6 We paid them for the goods $4,000.
7 It pays to be nice to your boss.

USING A DICTIONARY

A good dictionary doesn't just say what a word means.
It also provides information on pronunciation, grammar, and usage.

Pronunciation

/peɪ/ shows the individual sounds the word is made up of. Look for notes on how to pronounce the phonetic symbols at the front or back of the dictionary. In long words, the stress is marked. For example in *payment* /'peɪmənt/, the sign ' indicates that the first syllable is stressed.

Grammar

You can find out from the dictionary whether a word is a noun, verb, adjective (*adj*), etc. As *pay* is an irregular verb, the form of the past tense and past participle (*paid*) is also shown.

(U) indicates an uncountable noun — a noun with no plural form. Other examples are *money* and *information*. Countable nouns have a plural form, for example, *dollars, prices*.

(I) or (T) tells you if a verb is intransitive (has no object) or transitive (has an object). Some verbs can be both. Examples: *I've paid the bill* (T), *I've paid* (I).

Usage

Look for notes that give extra information about how a word is used, such as information about other words with similar meanings. Studying the examples sentences and phrases will help you to use the word correctly.

SKILLS WORK

Speaking 1

Negotiating tips

1 A negotiation is a business discussion between people who have different interests. During a negotiation they try to solve a problem or reach an agreement. What sort of negotiations do you take part in in your job?

2 Here are three pieces of advice for people who are entering a negotiation. Do you agree with them?

1 If you can't agree, try approaching the problem from a different angle.
2 Don't get emotional. Be objective.
3 Prepare carefully beforehand.

Which tip do you think is least useful and which is most useful?

3 Working individually, think of three more useful tips for negotiating. Write them down on three different pieces of paper.

4 Now get together with some colleagues. Examine the tips you have all written. As a group, select the three you think are most useful.

5 When you were deciding which tips to choose, did you all agree at once or did you have to negotiate? During the negotiations, did you follow any of your tips? Were they useful?

Speaking 2

A negotiation

1 Work with a partner. You are interested in doing business with one another. Set the scene. Decide what companies you represent. Who is the customer/client and who is the supplier? What goods or services are you buying and selling?

2 Set the agenda for a meeting to discuss the deal. Here are some points you may need to discuss. Think of some more and add them to the list.

The goods/services
- exactly what they are
- any accessories or extras
- quantities
- guarantees

Delivery
- timing
- method of transport
- insurance
- who will pay what

Payment
- price
- credit period
- discounts
- penalties for late payment/late delivery/cancellation/etc.

3 Consider the different positions of the supplier and client/customer. What problems will you each have to solve in the meeting? What concessions could each side want? For example,

- long credit period (customer)
- payment on delivery (supplier)
- 5-year warranty (customer)

4 Now hold your meeting and try to strike a deal. Good luck!

Listening

1 Jennifer D'Abo used to run Ryman, a successful chain of office stationery shops. Listen to her account of a problem she once faced. Stop the tape when you hear a short beep.

1 What exactly was the problem?
2 What would you do if you had this problem?
3 What do you think Jennifer did? Listen and find out.

2 Now listen to three more managers talking about problems they faced. In each case, stop the tape when you hear a short beep. Say how you would deal with the problem, then listen to find out what the manager did.

3 The managers used a lot of idiomatic expressions. Can you explain what they mean?

1 I'd had enough.
2 It ran like clockwork.
3 It frightened the life out of them.
4 They wouldn't budge.
5 They signed on the dotted line.
6 I hadn't a clue.

OBJECTIVE

to exchange factual information accurately and precisely

TASKS

to deal with queries about an invoice

•

to make travel enquiries

•

to spell and note down English words over the phone

•

to check and correct factual information

•

to give effective explanations by paraphrasing

•

to place and deal with orders over the phone

PRESENTATION

1 ▭ You are going to hear two people talking about this invoice. Listen to their conversation and circle the items the Spanish manager queries. Make a note of any necessary changes.

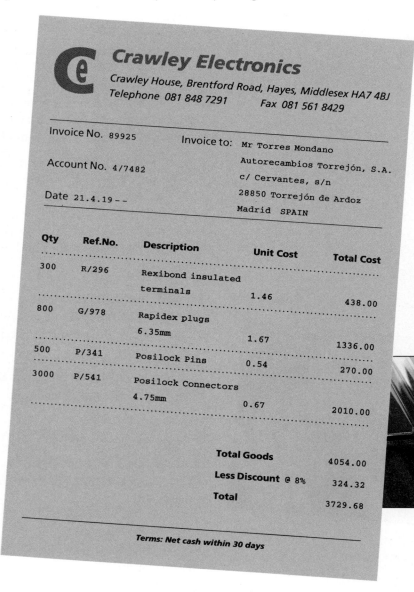

Crawley Electronics

Crawley House, Brentford Road, Hayes, Middlesex HA7 4BJ
Telephone 081 848 7291   Fax 081 561 8429

Invoice No. 89925

Account No. 4/7482

Date 21.4.19 – –

Invoice to: Mr Torres Mondano
Autorecambios Torrejón, S.A.
c/ Cervantes, s/n
28850 Torrejón de Ardoz
Madrid SPAIN

Qty	Ref.No.	Description	Unit Cost	Total Cost
300	R/296	Rexibond insulated terminals	1.46	438.00
800	G/978	Rapidex plugs 6.35mm	1.67	1336.00
500	P/341	Posilock Pins	0.54	270.00
3000	P/541	Posilock Connectors 4.75mm	0.67	2010.00

Total Goods	4054.00
Less Discount @ 8%	324.32
Total	3729.68

Terms: Net cash within 30 days

2 🔲 Now listen again and complete these extracts from the presentation.

Extract 1

A I've only received one so far. Could you tell me when
_____ ?

B On the twenty-first.

A And do you know _____ the Rapidex plugs?

B Yes, 800, reference number G978.

Extract 2

A Now the next thing is the Posilock connectors.

B They were in the first shipment, _____ on the 17th.

A Yes, they've arrived, but we ordered 3,500, not 3,000.

B Oh dear. I don't know _____ . We'll send the rest immediately. _____ ?

A Yes. I also wanted a word about our discount. _____ when I placed the order said we might be able to have 10%, not 8%.

B I'm afraid I'm not authorized to change it. Mrs Cusimano's the person _____ , and I'm afraid she's not here at the moment.

A Have you any idea _____ ?

3 Can you pronounce the English alphabet? What letters do you have difficulty in remembering?

4 Complete this pronunciation reference chart. Go through the alphabet saying each letter and deciding which column to put it in. (The first three have been done for you.)

Sound 1	Sound 2	Sound 3	Sound 4	Sound 5	Sound 6	Sound 7
/eɪ/	/iː/	/e/	/aɪ/	/əʊ/	/uː/	/ɑː/
as in *page*	*see*	*ten*	*five*	*home*	*too*	*arm*
A	B					
	C					

You can check your answers in File 13 on page 156.

LANGUAGE WORK

Pronunciation **1** ▭ Listen to the conversation and note down an address.

2 The woman spelt the word *Avenida* twice. What letter did she stress the second time and why?

3 ▭ Now listen to some more people checking their spelling. Look at the correct spellings below and circle the letters they get wrong. Then read the correct spelling back to them.

1 Mrs Kulesza
2 Maihar
3 Mr Ranjit
4 Harray
5 Ms Avelon

Checking and correcting **1** We use a lot of standard phrases to check information. Make yourself a handy checklist for future reference. Study the table, then add these phrases.

Was that ...?
Can I read that back to you?
OK?
Was there anything else?
Yes, fire away.
Yes, that's it.
No, I said ...

	Questions	Replies
Checking the other person's ready	Ready?	.... No, hang on.
Checking something they said	Did you say... ?	Yes, that's right. ....
Checking there's nothing more to say	Is that everything?	.... No, there's one more thing.
Checking you've got everything right	Could we run over that again?	Of course. Certainly. Sure.

2   Now practise the phrases in telephone conversations with a partner. One person should look at the information below and the other should look at the information in File 4 on page 151.

Call 1

There is an article about your company in one of your trade papers. Unfortunately, it contains a lot of mistakes. Phone the editor and complain. Explain what it should have said.

1   They misspelt your company's name.
2   They said your company's share price fell by 12% last month. In fact it rose by 15%.
3   They misspelt the name of one of your products.
4   They said your company's headquarters are in Chicago, USA.
5   They misspelt the name of your company's Chairman.

Call 2

You are the publisher of an international directory of famous business people. Someone calls you about some mistakes in their entry. Make a note of the errors so you can make corrections before the next printing.

Documents

1   Companies use different procedures and documents when buying and selling goods and services. These documents could all be sent by a buyer or a seller during the course of a sales transaction. Do you know what they are? Who would send them — the buyer or the seller?

☐ cheque   ☐ letter of enquiry
☐ order   ☐ invoice
☐ receipt   ☐ quotation
☐ delivery note   ☐ reminder

Number them in the order that they would normally be sent.

2   Work with a partner. What different things do we do with these documents? Brainstorm different verbs (actions) that you could use with each one in the list.

*You can **send** a letter of enquiry.*
*You can **receive** a letter of enquiry.*

When you have finished, you can compare your ideas with the suggestions in File 9 on page 154.

Explanations **1** Can you match these words to their explanations?

1	Karoshi (Japanese)	7	Kamaki (Greek)
2	Namaste (Hindi)	8	Fasching (German)
3	Sköl (Danish)	9	Mall (North American)
4	Mafioso (Italian)	10	Shadchan (Yiddish)
5	Ramadan (Arabic)	11	Ombudsman (Swedish)
6	Fung shui (Chinese)	12	Bortsch (Russian)

a   A month of the year when Muslims fast between sunrise and sunset.

b   Someone who belongs to a secret criminal organization.

c   A festival time when people wear funny clothes to work and visit beer gardens in the evening.

d   Death which is caused by overwork.

e   A covered area or building where there are many shops.

f   A person who arranges marriages.

g   A soup that's made from beetroot and cabbage.

h   A greeting where you put your palms together and bow.

i   A person whose job it is to investigate complaints made by individuals about government authorities.

j   Wind and water spirits which must be kept happy when a new building is erected.

k   Something people say to each other when they are having an alcoholic drink.

l   A national 'sport' where young men pick up female tourists.

When you have finished, you can check your answers in File 8 on page 153.

2   *Ramadan is a month of the year* **when** *Muslims fast between sunrise and sunset.*

When introduces the phrase that describes the time. Look through the other explanations and find similar words. What words introduce phrases that describe

- a person? (find one word)
- a thing? (find two words)
- a place or activity? (find one word)
- something a person has or possesses? (find one word)

3   The words in Exercise 1 were all connected with the customs and culture of different countries. Think of similar words in your language. How could you explain them to a foreign visitor?

4 Now try explaining the meaning of some English words. Complete this crossword with a partner. One person should use the information below and the other should use the information in File 16 on page 157.

There are no clues to this crossword, but you have half the answers and your partner has the other half so you need to explain the words to each other. You can say anything you like to help your partner, but of course, you mustn't say the missing words.

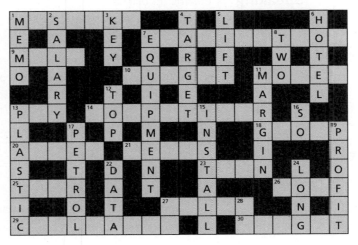

Enquiries

Indirect questions are a polite way of asking for information. We often use them at the start of a conversation. Notice how the word order differs from direct questions.

What time does the switchboard close down?
Could you tell me what time the switchboard closes down?

What's the code for Tokyo?
Can you tell me what the code for Tokyo is?

Should I dial 0 for an outside line?
Do you know | whether | I should dial 0 for an outside line?
* | if |*

Change the following questions into indirect questions. Practise asking and answering them with a partner. (You can invent the answers.)

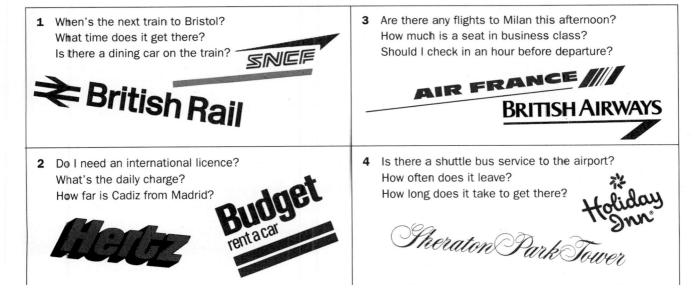

1 When's the next train to Bristol?
What time does it get there?
Is there a dining car on the train?

SNCF

≥ **British Rail**

2 Do I need an international licence?
What's the daily charge?
How far is Cadiz from Madrid?

Hertz **Budget** rent a car

3 Are there any flights to Milan this afternoon?
How much is a seat in business class?
Should I check in an hour before departure?

AIR FRANCE ////
BRITISH AIRWAYS

4 Is there a shuttle bus service to the airport?
How often does it leave?
How long does it take to get there?

Holiday Inn

Sheraton Park Tower

SKILLS WORK

Speaking

Placing an order

Work with a partner. One person should look at the information below and the other should look at the information in File 7 on page 153.

You work for MacWarehouse, a computer goods mail order company that offers some of the best deals around. A customer phones you. Use the information from your catalogue and make a note of their order.

Microsoft Excel 4.0

Believe it or not, you can actually create a spreadsheet in just about 60 seconds with Microsoft Excel 4.0. New intuitive features replace the long, steep learning curve with quick and powerful commands that have you up and running in a flash! Excel 4.0 gives you even greater control over how your finished documents will look. It provides everything you need to create dazzling reports, complete with charts, graphs, and notes or annotations.
Publisher: Microsoft
BUS 0223 **£219⁹⁵**

QuarkXPress 3.1

QuarkXPress 3.1 adds numerous new functions to this layout application. With its Colors Palette, you can apply color to text, pictures, lines, box back-grounds, and frames, and specify two-color blends.
GAK 0071 **£575**
Publisher: Quark

DateBook

Gives you the most advanced scheduling and alarm features, making it easier to plan and organize your work, and your life.
YWI 0222
Publisher: After Hours
Software **£79**

Quickmail 2.5.1

Solve all your E-Mail problems in one convenient package. This software supports any combination of Macs, and PCs running DOS, Windows, or OS/2 without gateways.
Publisher: CE Software
QuickMail 2.5.1 – 10 user
UHX 0102 **£319**

Microsoft Word 5.1

Microsoft Word 5.1 brings many new user conveniences to this time-tested word processor. Up to 30 on-screen buttons execute complex chores such as adding bullets, creating tables, inserting drop caps, and printing envelopes.
ERQ 0059 **£219**
Publisher: Microsoft

TouchBASE PRO

TouchBASE PRO is a powerful, full-featured contacts database. Store information about personal and business contacts. Print envelopes, mailing labels, address books, listing reports and fax cover sheets.
WYI 0076 **£79**
Publisher: After Hours Software

SPECIAL OFFER!
TouchBASE and DateBook Bundle
BND 0150 **£99**

MORE FOR YOUR MAC...MORE FOR YOUR MONEY ™

MacWAREHOUSE®

Queens Road
Barnet, Herts EN5 4DL
0800 181 332 • 081 449 7113
FAX: 081 447 1696

Date ....
Order taken by ....
Received by   Phone ☐
                        Fax ☐
                        Letter ☐

QUANTITY	PRODUCT NO.	PRODUCT NAME	COST EACH	TOTAL

Reading

I Passing on information clearly is not always easy, and being precise and accurate is even more important when writing than when speaking.

These extracts are all statements taken from insurance forms. In each case, a car driver has tried to explain how an accident happened, but they have explained badly. Where have they gone wrong? Can you work out what they meant to say?

2 Have you ever had a car accident? Tell the class what happened. And have you ever put in an insurance claim? Tell the class what it was for. Be precise!

Glossary

a telegraph pole
a tall wooden pole used for supporting telephone wires

to collide
to hit somebody or something very hard while moving

a pedestrian
a person who is walking in the street (not travelling in a vehicle)

to swerve
to change direction suddenly

stationary
not moving

an intersection
a place where two or more roads meet and cross one another

a bumper
a bar fixed to the front and back of a motor vehicle to reduce the effect if it hits something. (US English: *fender*)

a ditch
a long narrow hole in the ground at the side of a road or field

1
In an attempt to kill a fly, I drove into a telegraph pole.

2
Coming home, I drove into the wrong house and collided with a tree I don't have.

3
To avoid hitting the bumper of the car in front, I struck the pedestrian.

4
The indirect cause of the accident was a little guy in a small car with a big mouth.

5
A pedestrian hit me and went under my car.

6
I had been driving for 40 years when I fell asleep at the wheel and had an accident.

8
I collided with a stationary truck coming the other way.

7
The guy was all over the road. I had to swerve a number of times before I hit him.

9
As I approached the intersection, a sign suddenly appeared in a place where no stop sign had ever appeared before. I was unable to stop in time to avoid the accident.

10
The pedestrian had no idea which direction to run, so I ran over him.

11
I was thrown from my car as it left the road. I was later found in a ditch by some cows.

12
An invisible car came out of nowhere, struck my car and vanished.

OBJECTIVE

to take part in social conversations with foreign business contacts

TASKS

to make requests, offers, and invitations

•

to respond appropriately to a visitor's comments

•

to explain local customs to a foreign guest

•

to discuss cultural differences

•

to describe items on a menu for a foreign guest

•

to deal with problems encountered on a business trip

PRESENTATION

Client meeting on construction site in Kuwait

1 What foreign visitors do you welcome to your organization? Who are they and where do they come from? Do you ever go abroad to visit business contacts? What is the purpose of your trips?

2 ▭ You are going to hear five short conversations. Listen to each one and decide
• who you think the speakers are
• where they are
• what one speaker hands to the other.

3 Read these extracts from conversation 1. What do you think the missing words and phrases are?

A _____ have your name?

B _____ . Here's my card.

A Right, Mrs Sandbulte. _____ take a seat?

B I'm in a hurry, actually. _____ go straight up? I know the way.

A _____ you'll need security clearance first.

▭ Listen again and check your answers.

4 ▭ Listen to conversation 2 again then act out a similar conversation with a partner.

Host/hostess
Open the door, invite the guest in and take their coat.

Guest
Apologize for being late, explain why and give a present.

New products on display

5 If someone says 'Thank you', how can you reply? Think of as many different answers as you can.

Suppose they buy something for you and you want to refund them. What can you say?

▭ Now listen to conversation 3 again and compare your answers.

6 You are playing golf with someone and they play a good shot. What could you say? And what about if they make a bad shot?

Complete these sentences with the correct form of the verb in brackets.
1 I'm not usually very good at _____ (hit) those long shots.
2 I expect you're looking forward to _____ (get) back to Michigan.
3 You mustn't leave without _____ (visit) our plant there.
4 I'm interested in _____ (see) what you're doing there.

▭ Now listen to conversation 4 again and check your answers.

7 Read these extracts from conversation 5. What do you think the missing words are?

A I'm thinking of _____ my stay by a couple of days.
_____ you check if it's OK?
B Certainly.
A I'm Mrs Haberland, room 312.
B One moment.
A Instead of _____ on the fourteenth, I'd leave on the sixteenth.
B That's no problem. _____ I change the booking for you?

▭ Now listen to conversation 5 again and check your answers.

8 In some English expressions, we use a preposition followed by a gerund. A gerund is a noun made from a verb by adding *-ing*. Invent your own endings for these sentences. Use a gerund.
When I leave a party, I always thank the host or hostess for having me.

1 I never leave the office without _____
2 I'm looking forward to _____
3 I think I'll study this book tonight instead of _____
4 I'm interested in _____
5 Our customers insist on _____
6 I'm thinking of _____
7 If I've had a difficult day at the office, I often feel like _____
8 I'm very good at _____

LANGUAGE WORK

Polite phrases

1 All these modal verbs are used to make requests in English. Which ones could be used in the requests below?

could	may	would	can	will

1 .... you call me a taxi?
2 .... I use your phone?

For more examples of polite expressions, see page 184 of the Grammar and Usage notes.

2 We are generally quite formal when we are welcoming visitors to a company, so you would never hear any of the conversations below.

Work with a partner. Act out the same situations, using more formal language.

1 **Visitor**   I want to see Erling Lund.
  Receptionist   Tell me your name.
  Visitor   Kate Williams. Tell him I'm in a hurry.
  Receptionist   He's busy. Sit down there and wait.

2 **Receptionist**   Sign the visitor's book.
  Visitor   OK. Give me your pen.
  Receptionist   All right. Coffee?
  Visitor   I don't drink coffee. I want tea.

3 **Visitor**   Put my briefcase somewhere safe.
  Secretary   OK.
  Visitor   I want another cup of tea.
  Secretary   Pour it yourself, then.

4 **Visitor**   I want to see your customer address list.
  Client   You can't. It's confidential.
  Visitor   Your colleague, Mr Lopez, said I could.
  Client   Then he was wrong.

Pronunciation

The words you choose when you are speaking to foreign business contacts are very important. It wouldn't be polite to say
Tell me your name.

You need to use request forms like
May I have your name?
Could you tell me your name?

So the words are important. But the way you say them is also important. You need to use polite intonation.

1 ▭ Listen to an English sentence, spoken twice. The words are the same but the first one sounds polite and the second one sounds rude. Can you hear the difference?

2 ▭ Listen to some more sentences which are spoken twice. In each case, decide which version, a or b, sounds rude and which one sounds polite.

1 Would you mind waiting a moment?
2 May I have another cup of coffee?
3 Can you pour it yourself?
4 I'm afraid I'm in a hurry.
5 Would you call me a taxi?

Showing interest

1 Visitors from abroad may be interested to learn more about your country and local customs. For example, they might be interested in

- festivals
- the climate
- natural resources
- history
- races
- television and radio networks
- politics
- the economy
- the tax laws
- food and drink
- national sports
- the currency.

Work with a partner. Think of some questions that a visitor might ask you. Write them down.

2 Now take it in turns to ask and answer the different questions. The 'visitor' should show they are interested by asking more questions and making positive noises.
Yes?
That's interesting.
Really?
Mmm.
Oh.

3 You can show interest in your visitors by asking questions about their trip like this.

A *Have you been to Lyon before?*

B *Yes, I have. Just the once.*

A *Really? Was it a business trip or a holiday?*

B *I came to see a client, but I didn't stay long, unfortunately.*

Notice the tenses the speakers use. Why do they change from the present perfect to the past simple?

GRAMMAR NOTE

We can use both the past simple and the present perfect tense to talk about actions that happened in the past and are finished. We use the present perfect if we do not know (or are not interested in) when they happened.

I've been to Alicante several times.

And we use the past simple tense if we are referring to a definite occasion.

There was a big exhibition the last time I went.

---

4 Complete these questions you could ask a visitor, then use them to begin conversations with a partner. Remember to change to the past simple tense when you start talking about a definite time or occasion.

1 Have you visited .... before?
(your company)

2 Have you met .... yet?
(one of your colleagues)

3 Have you been to .... before?
(your town)

4 Have you seen .... ?
(an interesting building or place)

5 Have you ever tried .... ?
(a local dish)

6 Have you had a chance to try any .... before?
(a local drink)

Socializing

1 How could you reply to these comments? Think of different alternatives.

2 Now match these replies to the correct comment.

a I hope it goes well for you.

b Nothing serious, I hope.

c You poor thing.

d That's nice. How long are you going for?

e Congratulations! That *is* good news.

f What a pity. Some other time perhaps.

g Cheers!

h Oh dear. When did you last have them?

i Why? What happened then?

j Why? What's wrong with it?

Cultural differences

Language mistakes can cause problems when we're doing business with people from other countries. But communication can also break down when we misunderstand the way another culture works. In this task, you will be considering how behaviour can vary between cultures.

1 You are all attending an international conference and meeting people who come from many different cultures. Stand up, walk around the room, and talk to the other conference participants. You can talk about anything you like: whether they are enjoying the conference, what talks they have been to, their work, their family, hobbies, holidays, sports — anything at all. However, you need to follow some rules.

Everyone's rules are different and they are at the back of the book. Different people should turn to the following files.

File 11 on page 155 (Culture A)
File 15 on page 157 (Culture B)
File 18 on page 158 (Culture C)
File 22 on page 159 (Culture D)
File 20 on page 158 (Culture E)
File 17 on page 157 (Culture F)

2 Describe any unusual behaviour you noticed at the conference. What sort of culture did you think the other people came from? Ask them if you were right.

How did their behaviour make you feel when you were speaking to them? How did they feel about your behaviour?

3 Discuss some of the cultural differences you have experienced in your working life. For example, differences in
- social distances and touching
- gestures
- how loudly people speak
- eye contact.

Muslims washing
before prayer

Traditional greeting, Dubai

Traditional greeting,
Rajasthan, India

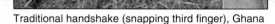

Traditional handshake (snapping third finger), Ghana

Sharing wine bowl,
Nigeria

SKILLS WORK

Speaking The Travel Game
Play this game with a partner. You are both going on business trips to visit foreign clients. The first person to complete their trip is the winner. Toss a coin to move: heads – move one square, tails – move two. Follow the instructions in each place you visit. Good luck and *bon voyage*!

Listening   **1**   How good is your restaurant vocabulary? How many words do you know? Test yourself with these questions.

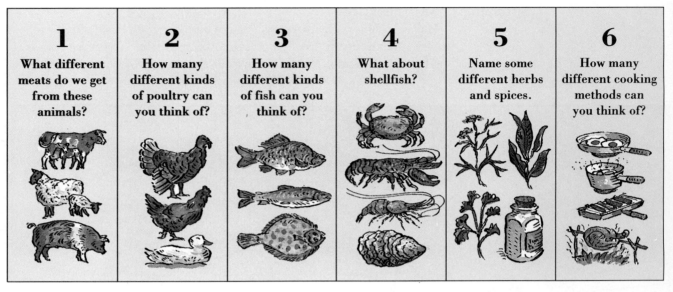

1	2	3	4	5	6
What different meats do we get from these animals?	**How many different kinds of poultry can you think of?**	**How many different kinds of fish can you think of?**	**What about shellfish?**	**Name some different herbs and spices.**	**How many different cooking methods can you think of?**

2   Study the restaurant menu on the opposite page. Find the names of

1   some fruits
2   some vegetables
3   a poultry dish
4   a fish dish
5   a shellfish
6   a herb
7   a spice
8   some different cooking methods.

What would you choose from the menu?

3   ▭   You are going to hear two people discussing what to eat at a business lunch at Dartford Lodge. Listen to their conversation and make a note of what they decide to order.

The man is going to have _____
The woman is going to have _____

4   Notice how we explain things by type.
Prawns are a type of shellfish.
Turbot is a kind of flat fish.
Oatmeal is a sort of flour.

Describe what these things are in a similar way.
• blackcurrants
• parsley
• lettuce

DARTFORD LODGE
HOTEL & RESTAURANT

Soup of the Day

Galia Melon
Chilled and served on crushed ice with a blackcurrant sorbet

Savoury Pancakes
With spinach and stilton

Avocado Pear
On a nest of lettuce leaves, garnished with prawns

*

Fillet of Turbot
Dusted with oatmeal and served with a parsley sauce

Lamb Cutlets
Charcoal grilled and served with mustard and tomatoes

Beef Wellington
Scottish beef with mushroom purée in a crisp pastry case

Breast of Chicken
Stir-fried and served with beanshoots and ginger

*

**A Choice of Desserts from the Sweet Menu
British and Continental Cheeses**

*

Coffee with Hand-Made Chocolates

5　We sometimes make adjectives (words that describe things) by adding -*y* to a noun, e.g. *leafy* (like a leaf).

How could you describe
- a dish that contained a lot of salt?
- a meal that contained a lot of fat?
- a wine that tasted of vinegar?
- a whisky that tasted of smoke?

6　Study the different prepositions in these sentences.
*The sauce is **made of** butter and parsley.*
*Oatmeal is **made from** oats.*
*Porridge is **made in** Scotland.*
*The chocolates are **made by** hand.*
*The menu is **made up of** starters, main courses, and desserts.*

Take an object from your briefcase, or choose an object in the room and make up sentences about it, using the expressions in **bold** print.

7　Think of some of the typical dishes of your country or region. Describe what they are like to a foreign visitor. Say what they are made of and how they are cooked.

OBJECTIVE

to report on progress
made in business
affairs

TASKS

to talk about recent
developments and
innovations

•

to analyse the financial
results of a company

•

to exchange
information about
your recent work
activities and
achievements

•

to give an account of
improvements in your
organization's results

•

to follow the radio
business news

PRESENTATION

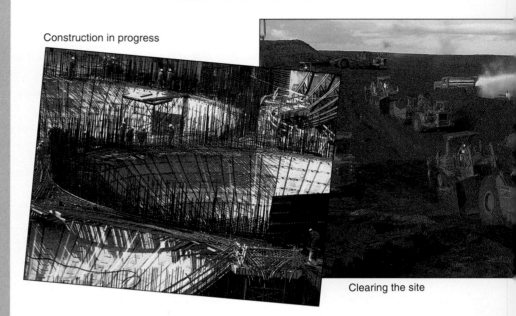

Construction in progress

Clearing the site

I   What do you think this chart refers to? What could the symbols represent?

DESCRIPTION	WEEK NUMBER														
	1	2	3	4	5	6	7	8	9	10	11	12	13	14	15
OFF-SITE PREPARATION	FEASIBILITY STUDY ▼														
ON-SITE PREPARATION						SITE PREPARATION ●									
INSTALLATION AND TESTS									INSTALLATION	TESTS ★					
PERSONNEL						RECRUIT OPERATORS		TRAIN OPERATORS							

MASTER PROJECT SCHEDULE

SYMBOLS
● =
▼ =
★ =

JOB NO.	COMPANY NAME
410/BA/944	INDEX ENGINEERING PLC.

2   ▭ Now listen to some managers discussing the schedule of a project and see if you were right.

Find out
1   what events the symbols represent
2   what week it is now
3   how they change the schedule

Engineer and site workers discuss plans

The drawing-board stage

3 🔲 Listen again and answer these questions.

1 What did the suppliers guarantee?
2 What did they do on schedule?
3 Whose fault is the delay?
4 What is happening with the operators at the moment?
5 What can't the company risk doing?

4 Complete these sentences from the conversation. Use either an infinitive or a gerund (*-ing*) form of one of the verbs from the box.

We planned ***to have*** this equipment in operation by week 12.

We dislike ***changing*** the schedule as much as you.

get	put	install	change	have
give	prepare	deliver		

1 They guaranteed _____ and install the equipment within five weeks.
2 We chose _____ the site ourselves.
3 They deny _____ problems with their parts.
4 Have they managed _____ started now?
5 They won't finish _____ the equipment until the end of week 11.
6 We can carry on _____ them theoretical training.
7 We can't risk _____ over to the new equipment without a full week of tests.
8 You want _____ it off for a week.

GRAMMAR NOTE

Some English verbs can be followed by an infinitive and some can be followed by a gerund. (A gerund is a noun made from a verb by adding *-ing*.) Compare these sentences.

We've decided to install the equipment.
NOT ~~We've decided installing the equipment.~~
Decide is followed by an infinitive.

We've finished installing the equipment.
NOT ~~We've finished to install the equipment.~~
Finish is followed by a gerund.

The bad news is there are no rules to help you know which verbs are followed by gerunds and which are followed by infinitives. The good news is you probably know a lot of them already. And it won't take long to learn the others.

See page 181 of the Grammar and Usage notes for a list of common verbs that are followed by a gerund or an infinitive.

LANGUAGE WORK

Developments
As governments around the world are introducing stricter environmental legislation, automobile manufacturers are investing heavily in the research and development of electric vehicles.

1 Read the first advertisement and find out how long electric vehicles have been around.

ADVERTISEMENT

Who said the electric car was a new invention?

An electric taxi recharging at a Detroit Edison station in 1916

At the Electric Light Convention of 1911 everyone was talking about standardizing plugs for electric vehicles. But the very next year the discussion was put on hold by a dazzling new invention—an electric starter for the gasoline-powered automobile. Then Henry Ford started mass production and gasoline conquered the market.

But not for much longer. The electric vehicle is back on the road and once again you can fuel your car with safe, clean electricity. Detroit Edison is pleased to be a driving force behind the new technology.

So it's time to drive electric again and follow the road to a brighter future.

At the turn of the century, we supported fleets of electric vehicles: milk trucks, delivery vehicles, passenger cars. Downtown Detroit had four electric cab fleets charging at stations operated by the Edison Illuminating Company, the forerunner to Detroit Edison.

Detroit Edison
A good part of your life.

2 Here are the answers to some questions about the advertisement. Work with a partner. Write the questions.

1 No, it's an old invention.
2 At the turn of the century.
3 Four.
4 Standardizing plugs for electric vehicles.
5 He started mass production of the gasoline-powered automobile.

3 Electric vehicles have always been cleaner and quieter than gasoline-driven models, but they have their disadvantages too. What are they?

4 Read the second advertisement. Find out what it's for and what problems have been solved.

(ADVERTISEMENT)

THE EV BATTERY PROBLEM ENDS RIGHT HERE.

A two-part problem has long stalled the public acceptance of Electric Vehicles (EVs). The first part: lack of a powerful, lightweight battery. The second: technology to manufacture large quantities of that battery.

Electrosource has solved the first part of the problem. Independent tests have confirmed that the Electrosource HORIZON battery can be recharged 50% in less than 8 minutes (99% in 30). And HORIZON-powered EVs will go 100+ miles between charges.

And BDM Technologies, Inc. has solved the second part of the problem.

The HORIZON battery can be manufactured for significantly less than other advanced batteries (such as nickel iron varieties) and potentially for less than other lead acid types.

The future is on the HORIZON. We can bring it to you now. For further information, write Department 93, BDM Technologies, Inc., 7915 Jones Branch Drive, McLean, VA 22102. Phone 1-800-685-2361, Fax (703) 351-6909.

BDM TECHNOLOGIES
A BDM International Company

Electrosource Inc

THE SOLUTION STARTS RIGHT HERE.

5 Here are some answers to questions about the second advertisement. Work with a partner. Write the questions.

1 It's for a battery.
2 A two-part problem.
3 It has solved the first part of the problem.
4 That the Electrosource HORIZON battery can be recharged 50% in less than eight minutes.
5 Yes, BDM Technologies has.

6 Look back at the ad about the history of electric vehicles and highlight or underline all the examples you can find of the past simple tense. Then look at the ad for the battery and highlight all the examples you can find of the present perfect tense.

7 Study the examples of the two different tenses. What differences can you see in the way the tenses are used?

For more information on how to use the past simple and present perfect tenses, see pages 173 and 174 of the Grammar and Usage notes.

A social action programme

1 Have you ever heard of The Body Shop? Do you know anything about its policies?

2 Read about the organization's social action programme. Fill the spaces with the correct form of the verb in brackets. Use either the past simple or the present perfect tense.

FACT SHEET

The first branch of The Body Shop _____*opened*_____ (open) in 1976 in Brighton, England. We___*have now grown*___ (now grow) into a worldwide organization with more than 1000 stores. Since the very beginning, we _____ (be) committed to activities that benefit communities on both a local and global scale.

- Employees of The Body Shop are encouraged to take a half day's paid leave each month to participate in activities that benefit their local community. In 1991, we _____ (win) the UK Award for Employee Volunteering.

- We _____ (run) 21 campaigns to date, ranging from *Stop the Burning*, to protest about the destruction of Brazilian Rainforests, to human rights campaigns, run in association with Amnesty International. In 1990, 2.6 million people _____ (sign) our petitions against animal testing. In our Refill Recycle campaign in 1992, our customers _____ (bring) over 560,000 bottles back to our shops in the UK for refilling.

- In 1991, we (fund) _____ the launch of a newspaper, sold by homeless people who keep a proportion of the cover price. On the first day it _____ (sell) 10,000 copies. It _____ (now progress) from a monthly to a weekly newspaper, with a circulation of 135,000 copies per week.

- We _____ (start) a Romanian Relief Drive in 1990 to help abandoned children. So far, our project team _____ (renovate and refurbish) three orphanages and _____ (begin) care programs to improve the quality of the children's lives. Since the start we _____ (take care) to involve local people in our efforts and teams of volunteers _____ (work) alongside Romanian staff. In 1993, we _____ (expand) our efforts with another hospital project in Albania.

Ueno, Taitou-Ku, Tokyo, Japan.
First opened 31st August 1992

3 Discuss these questions with your colleagues.

1 The fact-sheet mentions four different sorts of activities that have helped communities. What are they?
2 The Body Shop's social action programme is highly unusual. What sort of corporate image do you think these activities create? Do you find it attractive?
3 The Body Shop prefers to invest in its social action programme rather than expensive advertising and promotion campaigns for its products. The programme benefits communities, but are there any commercial advantages?
4 Would you like your company to contribute to your local community or society at large in any way? If so, how?
5 Body Shop employees have taken part in a wide range of activities on their afternoons off, ranging from helping in local hospitals to cleaning up river banks. Would you like to be given time off to work in your local community? (What sort of work would you do?)

Reporting back

You're filling a colleague in on what happened at a meeting they missed. Complete the sentences below. Use the gerund or infinitive form of the verb in brackets.

The latest sales figures appear to be (be) down.
We risk losing (lose) our leading position in the market.

1 The domestic sales team have managed _____ (achieve) their targets ...
2 but the export sales team have failed _____ (reach) theirs.
3 The Sales Manager says she can't help _____ (be) worried.
4 She hopes _____ (get) better results next month ...
5 but says we can't avoid _____ (lose) sales ...
6 because our competitors keep on _____ (reduce) their prices.
7 She suggested _____ (lower) our prices too.
8 But the Marketing Director said we can't afford _____ (reduce) them.
9 He offered _____ (run) some special promotions next month ...
10 but refused _____ (cut) prices on a permanent basis.
11 So everyone delayed _____ (make) a decision.
12 We agreed _____ (wait) and see what happens next month.

Financial results

1 Study the balance sheet and profit and loss account on the opposite page. Find items that refer to

1 what the company owns and what it owes
2 things that permanently belong to the company
3 money they have to pay the bank for their loans
4 money borrowed to meet day-to-day running expenses
5 money supplied by shareholders
6 money owed to shareholders
7 money owed to suppliers
8 money their customers owe them
9 the company's total sales
10 costs incurred in buying raw materials and producing goods
11 expenses they've incurred but not yet received invoices for
12 regular expenses incurred in running the business such as rent, light, heating, salaries, and advertising expenses
13 the loss in value of equipment, etc., due to use or age
14 inventory.

2 Comment on some of the figures. Say which figures have gone up and which figures have gone down this year.

Investment income has gone down.
Debtors have risen.

Use as many different verbs (actions) as you can to describe the changes.

3 Work with a partner. The company has had a difficult year. Find evidence for these facts in the figures.

Fact: Competition has been very tough.
Evidence: Turnover has fallen.

Facts
• They've borrowed some money to buy new equipment.
• Their customers have been demanding that they keep larger stocks.
• Their customers have also been demanding longer credit periods.
• Their suppliers have been insisting on shorter credit periods.
• They've made some poor investments.
• And they haven't been able to afford to pay their shareholders much.

4 What about your company? What have your recent results been like?

INDEX ENGINEERING PLC

Balance Sheet as at 31st December

ASSETS	This year £'000	Last year £'000	LIABILITIES	This year £'000	Last year £'000
Fixed Assets			**Current Liabilities**		
Land and Buildings	301	648	Bank Overdrafts and Loans	1667	250
Plant and Equipment	631	507	Trade creditors	314	619
Investments	301	624	Accrued expenses	320	500
			Other Creditors including taxation	1043	890
	1233	1779	Dividend payable	70	160
				3414	2419
Current Assets			Net Current Assets / (Liabilities)	(594)	193
Stocks – Finished Goods	1296	800			
– Work in Progress	65	49			
Debtors	1086	880		639	1972
Cash and Bank	373	883			
	2820	2612	**CAPITAL AND RESERVES**		
			Share capital	200	200
			Profit and loss account	439	1772
				639	1972

INDEX ENGINEERING PLC

Profit and Loss Account for year ended 31st December

	This year £'000	Last year £'000
Turnover	4673	6219
Cost of sales	3875	2218
Gross Profit	798	4001
Administration and other Overheads	904	1452
Depreciation	362	202
Operating profit	(468)	2347
Investment income	105	596
Interest payable	(900)	(600)
Profit / (loss) on ordinary activities after tax	(1263)	2343
Dividends	70	160
Profit retained and transferred to reserves	(1333)	2183

Achievements

1 Have you ever heard of Procter & Gamble? What do you know about the company?

2 Read this statement about environmental quality management in Procter & Gamble. Why does Mr Artzt describe it as a never-ending journey?

Procter & Gamble is committed to improving the environmental quality of its products, packaging and operations around the world. This is not new for us. For decades we have been pursuing policies that will help protect, preserve and enhance the quality of the environment in which we all live.

The basis for our environmental systems and programs lies in the continuous improvement cycle. Environmental quality management is a never-ending journey.

All our divisions have achieved substantial improvements in their performance this year, but much lies ahead to be done.

Edwin L. Artzt
Edwin L. Artzt
Chairman and Chief Executive
The Procter & Gamble Company

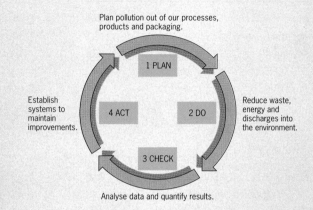

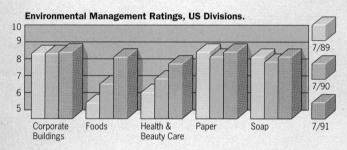

Environmental Management Ratings, US Divisions.

3 Find two examples of the present perfect tense in the statement. Why is the continuous form used in one and the simple form used in the other?

GRAMMAR NOTE

We use the present perfect simple to talk about completed actions.
We've analysed the data. (We've finished.)

But we use the present perfect continuous form to talk about actions over a period of time.
We've been analysing the data.
(We may or may not have finished.)

So we often use the continuous form with a phrase to say how long.
We have been pursuing these policies for decades.

And we often use the simple form with a phrase saying how much or many.
We've achieved a 50% reduction in waste.

4   Now work with a partner. Read about some of Procter & Gamble's achievements and make sentences about each one. Say what's been happening.

They've been transforming waste fibers into boiler fuel.

And say what savings they have made.

They've reduced solid waste by 75%.

Achievements using total quality for continuous environmental improvements

Pennsylvania pulpmill reduces solid waste

The P&G paper plant in Mehoopany, PA, transforms waste fibers into boiler fuel.
Saving: A 75% reduction in solid waste.

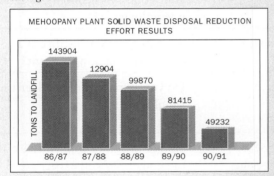

MEHOOPANY PLANT SOLID WASTE DISPOSAL REDUCTION EFFORT RESULTS

TONS TO LANDFILL

143904 — 86/87
12904 — 87/88
99870 — 88/89
81415 — 89/90
49232 — 90/91

Venezuela plant recycles waste water

P&G's Barquisimeto detergent plant now recycles water during the manufacturing process.
Saving: Enough water to supply 1000 people for a year.

Downy - a leader in source reduction

Ultra Downy is the first concentrated fabric softener available in a bottle made with at least 50% post-consumer recycled plastic.
Saving: Weight of packaging reduced by 35%.

London plant recycling

The London plant sorts plastic, cardboard and metals in its new indoor waste collection facility.
Saving: An 80% reduction in the amount of waste going into landfills.

Total Quality in Lima

Employees at the Lima detergent plant in Ohio use Total Quality tools to improve their processes and cut waste discharges.
Saving: Total waste cut by 77%.

New generation of detergents

Our new concentrated detergents such as Ultra Tide achieve the same level of cleaning with less bulk, while liquid detergent bottles are partly made with recycled plastic.
Saving: A 30% reduction in the packaging and chemicals used.

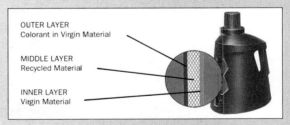

OUTER LAYER
Colorant in Virgin Material

MIDDLE LAYER
Recycled Material

INNER LAYER
Virgin Material

5   Now talk about your work in a similar way.

1   Make a list of some of the recent activities of your department, division or company.
2   Tell a partner about them. They should ask questions about how much work you have completed.

    A   *We've been getting ready to open a new sales office.*
    B   *What has that involved exactly?*
    A   *We've been taking on new staff and training them.*
    B   *How many new staff have you taken on and how much training have you given them?*

SKILLS WORK

Listening   **1**   🔘   You are going to listen to the radio business news. It's quite long and quite fast so don't expect to understand every word. While you listen, make brief notes on what the different news items are about.

2   Compare notes with a partner. Try to recall the subject of each item.

3   🔘   Listen again. Stop the tape at the end of each item and answer these questions.

	The news items	Your reactions to them
Item 1	What figures were mentioned? What were they for?	Would a cut in interest rates benefit your country's economy by reducing unemployment?
Item 2	Why do the workers feel the job cuts are unnecessary?	Are job cuts ever justified if a company is making a profit?
Item 3	What two organizations have issued reports recently? How have they conflicted?	Do you think cigarette advertising should be legal?
Item 4	What new retirement age does Mr Willett suggest? Why does he want to raise the pension age?	Should men and women retire at the same age? Do you expect your government to raise the pension age?
Item 5	What exactly is British Rail going to do to the volunteers and why? Who has volunteered so far and why?	How would you react if your employer asked you to take part in an experiment like this? Would you like to volunteer? Would you like to go bungee-jumping?

94

Pronunciation

Listen to these words. In each group there is one word that has a different vowel sound to the rest. Which one is it?

1	news	move	book	two
2	cut	suit	some	truck
3	won	but	met	touch
4	shoot	good	put	should
5	must	look	once	luck
6	spend	come	meant	left

Speaking

Business achievement award

The government is offering an award for business achievement to be given to the company, division or department that has done most to improve results in one of these areas.

- customer service
- productivity
- reductions in wastage rates
- staff training
- improvements in a process
- cost reductions
- environmental protection
- social and community action

Select one of the areas on the list where your company or department has improved results in the last twelve months. Prepare to give a presentation to the class. Describe

1 the results you aimed to improve
2 the goals you set yourselves
3 the measures you have implemented
4 how you have measured your progress
5 the results you have achieved.

The winner of the award will be the person or group who gives the best presentation.

OBJECTIVE

to describe changing
trends in your field of
business

TASKS

to describe changes in
your country's
economy

•

to exchange opinions
about the likelihood of
future events

•

to analyse the causes
and effects of social
trends

•

to write a divisional
performance report

•

to discuss changes in
your organization's
operating environment

PRESENTATION

1   Sales of some products are very seasonal. At what time of year would you expect these products to sell well?
- ice-cream
- fireworks
- umbrellas
- toiletries
- sun-tan lotion

2   You are going to hear a manager talking about market trends in the sales of sun-tan creams and lotions. Before you listen, look at the graphs and tables. What might they relate to?

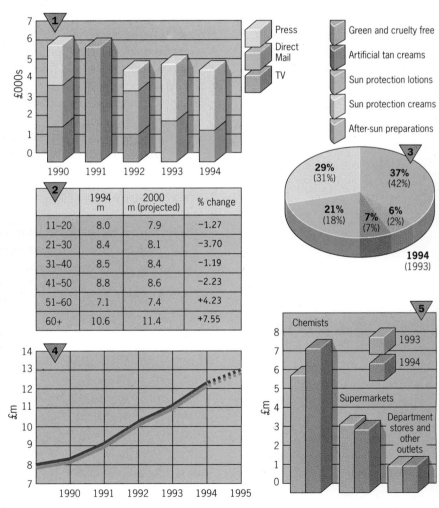

	1994 m	2000 m (projected)	% change
11–20	8.0	7.9	−1.27
21–30	8.4	8.1	−3.70
31–40	8.5	8.4	−1.19
41–50	8.8	8.6	−2.23
51–60	7.1	7.4	+4.23
60+	10.6	11.4	+7.55

3   Now listen to five extracts from the manager's presentation. Match each one to the correct graph or table.

4 Label each graph or table with one of these titles.
- Total sales
- Sales by sector
- Sales by distribution outlet
- Advertising budget / media spend
- Age shifts within the population

5 📼 Listen to Part 1 again. Make notes in the boxes to complete this causes and effects chain.

Now explain what has happened using these phrases from the presentation.

... is largely due to ...
... may be a result of ...

6 📼 Look at the graph showing sales by distribution outlet. Describe how sales have changed between this year and last year.

Now listen again. How does the presenter describe the changes?
Why have sales through chemists increased?

7 📼 Listen to Part 3 again and answer these questions.

1 What experiment did they do four years ago?
2 Was it successful?
3 What is the advantage of press advertising?

8 📼 Can you guess the missing words in these sentences?

_____ changes will _____ have an adverse effect on the market in the future. The population is ageing and it's _____ that this will have a _____ influence.

Listen to Part 4 again and check your answers. What words does the presenter use to describe the changes in size of the 21-30 and the 50+ age groups?

9 📼 Look at the pie chart showing sales by sector. Describe the relative size of the different product groups. How have they changed this year?
Then listen again and see how the presenter describes the changes.

LANGUAGE WORK

Discussing probability **1** Study some of the expressions we use to talk about how probable future events are.

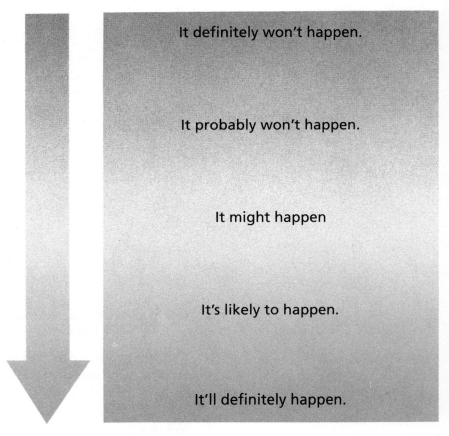

It definitely won't happen.

It probably won't happen.

It might happen

It's likely to happen.

It'll definitely happen.

Position these expressions in the correct place on the line.

1 It could happen.
2 It'll probably happen.
3 It isn't likely to happen.
4 There's no chance of it happening.
5 It's bound to happen.
6 It may happen.

Now position these opinions about the future on the line.

a I'm sure it'll happen.
b I think it'll happen.
c I doubt if it'll happen.
d I expect it'll happen.
e I don't think it'll happen.
f I don't doubt that it'll happen.

For help with constructing sentences using these different forms, look at page 177 of the Grammar and Usage notes.

2 Talk to some colleagues. Find out how likely they think the events below are. Use as many different expressions as you can to show how certain you feel.

A *Do you think we could have another Gulf war?*
B *I'm afraid we might. What do you think?*
A *I doubt if we will.*

1 We have another Gulf war.
2 Your company makes a loss.
3 Interest rates go down.
4 You get a job abroad in the future.
5 The rate of unemployment rises.
6 Demand for your products or services increases.
7 Your company makes staff redundant.
8 China becomes a major economic power.
9 There is a woman in the top position in your company.

Market movements

1 Here are some common verbs (actions) that we use to describe changes in a market. Do they describe upward or downward movements? Are they regular or irregular verbs? Complete the chart.

STEM	MOVEMENT	PAST	PAST PARTICIPLE
increase	↗	increased	increased
decrease			
fall			
rise			
raise			

2 Underline the verbs in these sentences.

Prices rose sharply.
Our suppliers raised their prices sharply.

Notice how the verbs are used differently. In both sentences the prices went up. But in the first sentence they went up on their own. In the second sentence someone put them up.

Complete these sentences with the correct form of the verbs *raise* or *rise*.

1 The Chancellor has just _____ the duty on petrol.
2 The sun _____ in the east and sets in the west.
3 Our share price has _____ recently.
4 She _____ an important point at the meeting yesterday.
5 Bank lending rates _____ by 0.5% last month.
6 Could I _____ a question?

3 Here are some newspaper headlines. Are they good news or bad? Highlight or underline verbs that indicate a movement. Is it upwards or downwards?

Pepsi Co. sales jump

Land prices soar

SHARE PRICES TUMBLE

Truck sales plunge

CEO wages rocket

CAR PRICES SLUMP

PUBLIC SECTOR SPENDING TAKES OFF

4 Here are some more newspaper headlines. What stories do you think they are about?

a **PLANS TO SHRINK NAVY**

b **Trade deficit improves**

c **DOLLAR WEAKENS**

d **Losses double at Big Blue**

e **PACE OF RECOVERY GAINS MOMENTUM**

Underline all the verbs in the headlines. Can you think of verbs with the opposite meaning? For example,

double $\neq$ *halve*

Which of these verbs can you make into a noun? For example,

to weaken (verb) ⟶ *weakness* (noun)

Pronunciation The word *increase* can be a noun or a verb. The stress falls on the first syllable if it is a noun (a thing) and the second syllable if it is a verb (an action).

We need an increase in output.
We need to increase our output.

1 Here are some more words that follow this pattern. Try saying each word twice. Change the stress each time.

decrease   import   export
progress   record   refund

2 Now listen to the words in sentences and mark which syllable is stressed.

Describing changes

1 Label the graph using these descriptions.

1 a dramatic increase
2 a steady rise
3 a peak
4 a trough
5 a sharp drop
6 a slight decline

Mark the places where sales

a remained stable
b fluctuated
c decreased substantially
d levelled off
e fell by 1,000 units
f fell to 1,000 units.

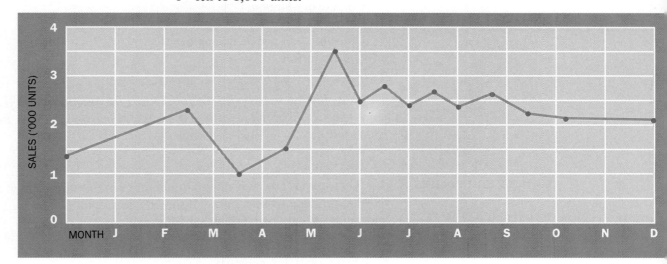

2 Work with a partner. Take it in turns to describe the graph.
There was a steady rise in sales in January and the first half of February, then they fell to 1,000 units in mid March.

Think of different ways to describe the changes.
Sales rose for the first six weeks of the year, then decreased substantially, and there was a trough in mid March.

3   These adjectives can all be used to describe changes.

slight   *steady*   *sharp*   *dramatic*
substantial   *rapid*   *gradual*   *negligible*

Some describe the size of an increase or decrease, some describe the rate or speed and some describe both.

A slight increase is a very small increase.
A steady increase is a regular increase. It isn't sudden.
A sharp increase is a large and sudden increase.

Look at the other adjectives and say what sort of changes they describe.

4   An adjective describes a noun and an adverb describes a verb.

There was a sharp increase in profits.   *Profits increased sharply.*

     adjective   noun   verb   adverb

Make adverbs from the list of adjectives in 3. Add *-ly* and make any other necessary changes in spelling. For example, *sharply, steadily.*

5   Try using some of the adjectives and adverbs to describe changing trends in your country. Work with a partner. Write sentences describing increases and decreases in these things.

1   The rate of inflation
2   Interest rates
3   The number of people unemployed
4   Property prices
5   Rates of direct and indirect taxation

The rate of inflation rose steadily for the first few months of the year but there's been a slight fall recently. I think it will remain steady for the next few months.

Causes and results   **1**   These trends are visible in many countries in the world today. Are they happening in your country? If so, why do you think they are happening? What do you think caused them?

• People are living longer than they used to.
• Jobless totals are increasing.
• The cost of imports is rising.
• Public concern about road accidents is growing.
• Governments are reducing expenditure on defence.
• People are becoming more aware of green issues.
• More students are taking higher education courses.

Where do you think these trends will lead? What will be the results?

2 Now match each trend to one of the causes and one of the results in these lists.

Causes

1 The shortage of jobs available for young people
2 Improved health care and medical advances
3 Rises in accident statistics
4 Political changes in the former Soviet Union
5 Currency devaluations
6 The publicity given to the effects of pollution
7 The economic recession

Results

a Stricter laws on drink-driving
b An increase in demand for environmentally-friendly goods
c Inflation
d A better qualified workforce
e Increasing numbers of pensioners
f Substantial increases in the costs of unemployment benefits
g A decline in the aerospace industry

Make sentences about each trend, describing how it came about and saying what the results will be. The phrases in the boxes will help you.

People are living longer now than they used to. This is largely due to improved health care and medical advances. As a result, we will have increasing numbers of pensioners in the population.

Explaining causes	Describing results
This is a result of ...	*As a result, we will have ...*
This is because of ...	*It could lead to ...*
This is largely due to ...	*It may result in ...*
... contributed to this.	*... will be a direct result.*

3 Draw a graph or table that shows a trend or changes in your industry. (Or bring one that you have at work into class.) For example, it could show

- increases/decreases in sales
- changes in staffing levels
- changing patterns of demand
- rising or falling costs or prices
- changing volumes of output.

Tell a colleague what it represents. Explain the changes, saying what the causes are and what the results will be.

SKILLS WORK

Writing   **1**   Read this report on the performance of the Laura Ashley Group. Underline all the phrases used to describe relationships between causes and their results.

Company Report

• •

The strong turnaround in Laura Ashley's results this year can be attributed to several factors. One of these was our new simplified management structure which led to faster decision-making processes and substantial cost reductions. A second factor was the increase in sales which resulted from new merchandising techniques and greater employee involvement.

However, in North America our performance was disappointing. This was largely due to unsatisfactory margins, brought about by problems with stock control and distribution. We expect significant changes in next year's results. Our new alliance with Federal Express will lead to better information systems and consequently an improvement in the flow of goods within our supply chain.

Laura Ashley shop, Cambridge

2   Write short notes in the empty boxes of this diagram to show the chains of events.

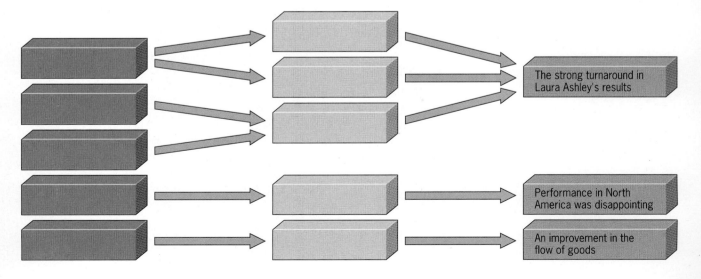

3 Use this diagram to write a similar report on the performance of the Chemicals Division of another company. Follow the same pattern.

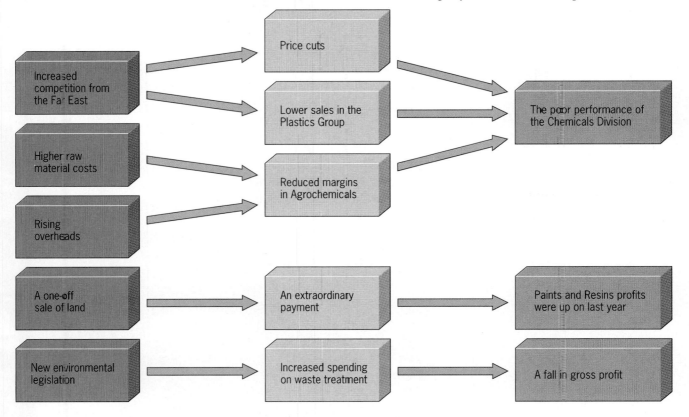

Speaking

A STEP analysis is a useful business tool for examining ways in which organizations need to adapt to changing external environments. STEP stands for sociological, technological, economic, and political changes. Perform a STEP analysis of your company or department. Discuss how your work is being affected (or may be affected) by these factors.

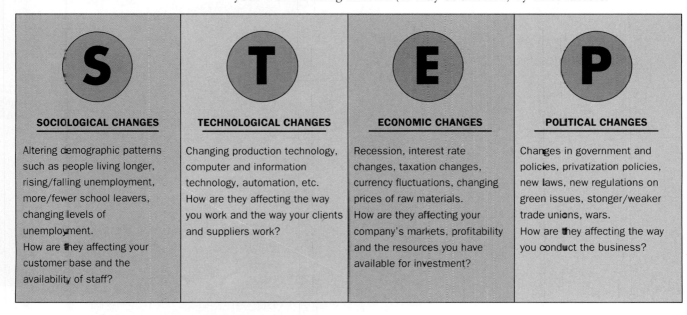

S	T	E	P
SOCIOLOGICAL CHANGES	**TECHNOLOGICAL CHANGES**	**ECONOMIC CHANGES**	**POLITICAL CHANGES**
Altering demographic patterns such as people living longer, rising/falling unemployment, more/fewer school leavers, changing levels of unemployment. How are they affecting your customer base and the availability of staff?	Changing production technology, computer and information technology, automation, etc. How are they affecting the way you work and the way your clients and suppliers work?	Recession, interest rate changes, taxation changes, currency fluctuations, changing prices of raw materials. How are they affecting your company's markets, profitability and the resources you have available for investment?	Changes in government and policies, privatization policies, new laws, new regulations on green issues, stonger/weaker trade unions, wars. How are they affecting the way you conduct the business?

OBJECTIVE

to describe a
company's products
and services

TASKS

to describe the
sequence of events in
a business process

•

to discuss a client or
customer's
requirements

•

to outline systems for
ensuring quality

•

to ask and answer
questions about
products and services

PRESENTATION

1 🔲 An electrical machinery manufacturer is employing the services of an engineering consultant to design a motor. Listen to the conversation and number these steps in the order they occur in the design process.

☐ Do some sketches
☐ Select the best options
☐ Write the specifications
☐ Draw up detailed designs
☐ Identify the design objectives
☐ Discuss the different options

2 Discuss the design process with a partner.

A *First the design objectives are identified.*
B *What's the next step?*
A *The specifications are written.*
B *What happens after that?*

3 Listen to the conversation again and answer these questions.

1 What must the new motor be like?
2 What design problems must the consultant solve?
3 At what stage will he provide a breakdown of costs?
4 How long will it take to get the sketches ready?

4 Complete this extract from the conversation. Use the words in the box.

| have to | must | don't have to | mustn't |

A The main problem will be the cooling system. It _____ be cooled by water.
B On the other hand, the working environment is clean. We _____ worry about dust and dirt.
A You _____ solve the vibration problem too.
B Yes, it _____ vibrate above the limits, but that needn't be a major problem.

What's the difference in meaning between *mustn't* and *don't have to*?

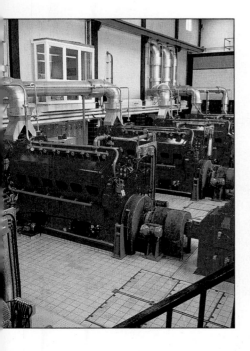

5 Now complete this extract from the conversation using the words in the box.

| be able | should | ought | can |

A _____ we meet again at that stage?
B Yes, we _____ to. Then I _____ show you the different options.
A Will you have price estimates by then?
B Yes, I'll _____ to give you a pretty accurate breakdown of costs.

Which verbs are always followed by *to*?
Which verbs have similar meanings?

LANGUAGE WORK

Pronunciation

1　▭ Listen to this conversation. Note the different ways *can* and *can't* are pronounced.

A Can you do it in a week?
B I'm afraid we can't.
A Can't you get someone to help you?
B We can, but it won't save much time. We can probably do it in two.

Can is pronounced /kæn/ when it is stressed.
Can is pronounced /kən/ when it isn't stressed.
Can't is pronounced /kɑːnt/ in British English and /kænt/ in American English.

2　Read the conversation with a partner. Pay attention to the pronunciation of *can* and *can't*.

Terms of business

1　Look at some of the different verbs we use to talk about ability and obligation.

must	mustn't	have to	don't have to
should	shouldn't	can	can't
ought to	have got to	need to	needn't

What do they mean? Which ones do we use to talk about actions that are

1 necessary?
2 not necessary?
3 good things to do?
4 bad things to do?
5 possible?
6 impossible?

You must do it — it's necessary.
You don't have to do it — it isn't necessary.

GRAMMAR NOTE

Must, *have (got) to* and *need to* all express strong obligation in their positive forms, but they have different meanings in their negative forms. *Mustn't* expresses an obligation *not* to do something. We use it to talk about things that are bad or prohibited. *Needn't* and *don't have to* express the idea of no obligation. We use them to talk about things that are not necessary. *Should*, *ought to*, and *shouldn't* express weak obligation, so we often use them to make suggestions.

2 Study these terms of business. Make a sentence or sentences explaining each one, using appropriate verbs.

Customers are respectfully requested to pay within 14 days.

You | should | *pay within 14 days.*
    | ought to |

You shouldn't pay later than 14 days.

1   Special offer. Save £££s.
2   Prices include carriage and VAT.
3   All fees payable in advance.
4   Rent or buy.
5   No credit card payments.
6   Please return the counterfoil with your payment.
7   Money-back guarantee.
8   Free delivery on orders over £100.
9   Payment within 30 days.
10 Available for immediate delivery.
11 30 days' free trial.
12 FREEFONE 0800 948024 to arrange for a FREE demonstration.
13 Make cheques payable to 'Action Reflex'.
14 Sale or return.
15 Don't delay. Limited offer. $500 off if purchased before 30 June.

3 Read this manager's comments on the credit his company gets.
A few years ago we could only get 30 days' credit from our suppliers. Recently we've been able to get 60 days' or more. It's all thanks to the recession. Companies couldn't risk losing business, so they had to offer better terms. It's been very good for our cash flow.

Underline all the verbs that express ability and obligation.

Can has a present form *(can)* and a past form *(could)*. What verb do we use in the other tenses?
Must has no past form. What verb do we use instead?

4 Practise the verbs with a partner. Think of
• some things you *could* and *couldn't* do when you were 20 years old
• some ways in which you've *been able to* practise English outside lessons
• some things you *had to* do before you came to your lesson today.

Meeting requirements

1 Who are your company's main customers or clients?

2 What products do you sell them? Think of adjectives that describe them.

advanced   high-quality   reliable

What services do you provide? Think of adjectives that describe them.

efficient   fast   professional

3 Why do your customers or clients buy from you rather than one of your competitors? Look at the list of points and decide how important they are for your customers.

Are they
- essential (E)?
- important (I)?
- unimportant (U)?

Write E, I or U in the boxes.

☐ Lower prices than anyone else
☐ Competitive prices
☐ Lengthy settlement terms
☐ Flexible payment arrangements
☐ Professional staff
☐ Specialized know-how
☐ Fast service
☐ Reliable delivery dates
☐ Large stocks carried
☐ Ability to meet quality standards
☐ A good after-sales service
☐ Ability to adapt products/services to meet special requirements
☐ A wide range of products/services
☐ A good reputation in your industry

4 Do you have any other factors to add to this list?

5 Compare your answers with a partner. Discuss what you have to do to ensure you meet your customers'/clients' requirements.

We don't have to offer lower prices than anyone else but our prices must be competitive.

Technical description

1 Read the pairs of texts and try to work out what piece of equipment each pair refers to.

A	B
1 You press this handle on top. Give it a hard push then point the spray at the flames.	The carbon dioxide has been stored under pressure. It is released when the lever is depressed.
2 You put the document under the flap. Key in the number of copies you want and then press the green button.	It was invented in 1938 by Chester Carlson. It's a dry process in which the powder is attracted by an electrostatically charged plate.
3 You need a 50p coin to put in the slot. It only buys two hours so you need to keep coming back and feeding it when the warden isn't looking.	The pointer is moved by clockwork to show the amount of time remaining. A penalty flag is raised when the time expires.
4 Look for the + and − signs, then you know which way up it goes. You can recharge it when it runs down.	An electric current is produced when the two terminals are connected to form a circuit.
5 The switch is on the steering column. You pull it towards you when you want them on full and back when you want to dip them.	Two concave mirrors have been placed behind the bulbs. Light rays are reflected by their curved surfaces to form two narrow bright beams.
6 You pin it to your tie then just speak at normal volume. You don't have to strain your voice.	A weak signal will be emitted which will travel to a mixer, then an amplifier and finally to a loudspeaker.

2 Compare the A texts with the B texts. Which ones

1 give instructions?
2 explain how things work?
3 are likely to be written?
4 are likely to be spoken?
5 are more informal?
6 are more technical?

Underline all the examples of the passive that you can find in column B.

GRAMMAR NOTE

In instructions, we often use *you* to talk about the people who will perform an action. *You* refers here to people in general, rather than a particular person.

In formal technical descriptions, the person who performs an action is generally not important and we often use the passive. For more information, see page 181 of the Grammar and Usage notes.

Total Quality Management

1 How does your company ensure the quality of its product or service? Do you employ Total Quality Management (TQM)?

2 Read what this consultant has to say about TQM. Do you agree with her?

The key to quality is very simple. You should do a job right first time. Most organizations do jobs approximately. They make mistakes that they have to fix later so they incur higher costs. In a TQM organization they know it's cheaper to do the job right in the first place.

So what does 'doing it right' involve? It means you mustn't waste resources; no wasted materials, no wasted time and no wasted space. And it means you have to throw out outdated processes. It's a constant and never-ending process and it has to involve everyone in the organization.

You have to push responsibility close to the point where employees and customers meet. It's your operating employees that have to make the important decisions because they're closest to the customers. And that means you have to stand the traditional management hierarchy on its head.

You must give employees more decision-making powers. Instead of giving them orders from above, your administration should support them and try to make their life easier. You can't do that in an atmosphere of conflict. You can only do it through creative teamwork.

3 So far the principles of TQM have been most widely used in manufacturing rather than service industries. Do you think they are applicable to service industries? Are they applicable to your business?

4 Your boss has asked for a report on TQM, giving a brief description of the principles behind it and your opinions on how it benefits, or could benefit, your organization. Complete the report below. Look back to what the consultant said to see what verbs to use. Put them into the passive.

INTERNAL REPORT

For the attention of: _____   **From:** _____

Date: _____   **Re:** Total Quality Management

1   The principles

TQM is a management philosophy. At its heart is the principle that a job _should be done_ [1] right first time. In most organizations, jobs _are done_ [2] approximately. Mistakes _____ [3] that _____ [4] later so higher costs _____ [5]. TQM organizations believe that it's cheaper if the job _____ [6] right in the first place. This means materials, time and space _____ [7] and outdated processes _____ [8]. It is a constant and never-ending process and everyone in the organization _____ [9].

Responsibility _____ [10] close to the point where employees and customers meet. So important decisions _____ [11] by the operating employees, because they are closest to the customers. That means the traditional management hierarchy _____ [12] on its head. Employees _____ [13] more decision-making powers. Instead of following orders from above, they _____ [14] by the administration who try to make their life easier. This _____ [15] in an atmosphere of conflict. It _____ [16] through creative teamwork.

2   The benefits

As regards the benefits TQM could bring our organization, in my opinion _____ _____ _____ .

5 Discuss the issue of quality in your organization. Ask and answer these questions with a partner.

1   What systems or processes do you have for ensuring the quality of your products or services?
2   What 'quality' training is given to staff?
3   How are operating staff encouraged to make improvements to processes and systems?
4   What is done to reduce waste?
5   How are results measured?
6   Are teams employed to deal with quality issues? How are they formed? How do they work?

SKILLS WORK

Speaking

1 Think of ten questions a customer or supplier could ask you about the product or service your company provides. For example, they could be questions about

- prices and payment
- delivery
- technical specifications
- quality standards
- how systems work
- procedures and processes.

Write the questions down.

2 Now give your questions to a colleague. They will ask them and you should answer.

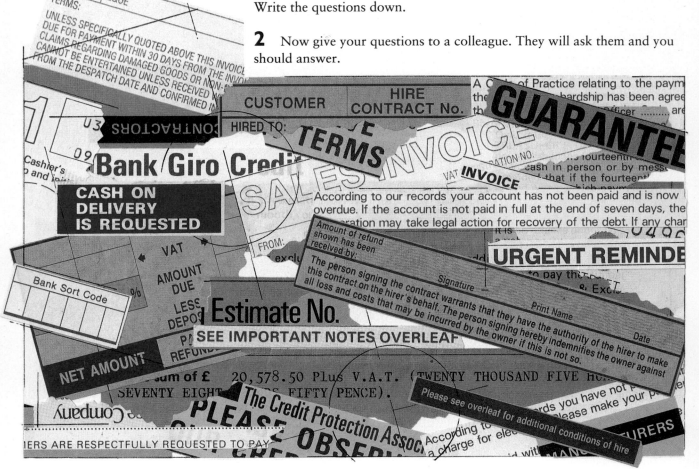

Reading

Reading is an excellent way of improving your vocabulary. But it isn't sensible to look up every new word you meet in a dictionary. You need to develop the habit of ignoring words you don't know and reading on. If necessary, you can often guess what words mean. This exercise gives practice in working out the meaning of unknown words.

1 Look through the article on the opposite page for 60 seconds to get a rough idea of what it is about. (Your teacher will time you.)

These boots are made for export

Every walker wants *waterproof* boots. They are the key to comfort, progress and even *survival*. Nick Brown, the *creator* of Nikwax, realized this at 15, cooked up his own solutions in the kitchen and at 21 discovered he had a *viable* product.

'I actually sold my first *tin* of Nikwax in 1977. I was going to Scotland and needed new boots. The guy at Alpine Sports in London sold me a pair and tried to sell me some *wax* too. I told him I made my own and why it was better. He took six dozen tins.'

Nick's company now sells a whole range of *rub-in*, *spray-on* and *wash-in* waterproofing products as well as waterproof clothing. Sales have increased at a steady 10 to 15 per cent a year and today the company employs five people, who all spend around 30 per cent of their time on research.

'When we started, the biggest problem was getting customers to buy large enough quantities. So I offered them advertising by printing their logo on the *lid* in exchange for a *minimum order*. Two things happened. First, the shops bought more, and second, because people who were satisfied with the product knew where to buy it, the shops with logos *outsold* the others.'

In the second year, he had a turnover of 50,000 units. He moved from his kitchen into a small *workshop*, making wax by night and selling it by day. He sold to outdoor shops all over the UK and he *interrailed* around the mountain centres in Europe, winning orders from the big names in boots, Fjellraven, Edelweiss and Kaufmann, Van de Sport. Le Trappeur, France's biggest manufacturer, ordered 60,000 tins. European sales *outstripped* those in the UK.

Nick believes strongly in research and international marketing. He is a linguist (an *ex-student* of the School of African and Oriental Studies) and he makes sure his foreign language publicity material is accurate to the last *accent*. Unlike most British companies, he invoices in local currency. 'I'd rather risk losing money on individual deals than losing a customer because *exchange rates* have changed.'

The big question now is whether outdoor shops can *survive* the *recession*. Four years of *drought* on top of economic decline have been bad for business. 'Now, thank God, it's raining,' says Mr Brown.

Nick testing the waterproofing powers of his TX10 Damp-proof wax.

2 Discuss what you have read with your colleagues. Tell them what you think the article is about.

3 Now read the article in more detail and see if you were right. With a partner, look at the words and phrases in *italic* print. Say what they mean. If you are not sure, try to work it out. Underline any other words you don't know and try to work out what they mean too.

4 Do you know any similar stories about how other businesses began? Tell them to the class.

GUESSING UNKNOWN WORDS

1 Suffixes

- The letters at the end of a word often indicate what type of word it is.

  *recess**ion***
  noun   (economic decline)

  *vi**able***
  adjective   (financially workable)

  *strong**ly***
  adverb   (in a strong way)

- *-proof* is a common suffix for adjectives. We use *waterproof* to describe something that water cannot penetrate. What things could these adjectives describe?

  sound-proof
  bullet-proof
  fireproof
  inflation-proof
  foolproof

2 Prefixes

- The prefix *inter-* means *between*. So *interrailed* means 'travelled by train (rail) between countries'. Can you think of any other words that begin with *inter-*?

- A *minimum order* is the smallest quantity of goods that can be ordered. So what does the prefix *mini-* mean? Think of more words that begin *mini-*.

- Nick is no longer a student. He is an *ex-student*. We can use the prefix *ex-* in front of other nouns that refer to people. Think of more 'people' nouns with the prefix *ex-*.

3 Word families

- Several English words can come from the same root. For example, the verb *to survive* (to continue to live) is related to the noun *survival*. What is a *survivor*?

- A *creator* is a person who makes or creates things. Think of more words that come from the same root as *creator*.

- Think of words that come from the same root as these words: *product, economic.*

- *Economic* and *economical* are both adjectives (words that describe things). What is the difference in meaning?

4 Word combinations

- Many English words are a combination of two other words. For example, *wash-in* means 'put in by washing'. How can we describe things that are

  1 put on by spraying?
  2 put in by rubbing?

- To *outsell* means to sell in larger quantities than another product, and to *outstrip* means to become of greater importance. Can you guess the meaning of these sentences containing *out-* combinations?

  3 The advantages of the proposal far *outweigh* the disadvantages.
  4 The only woman on the board was *outnumbered* nine to one.
  5 When they reduced their prices by 10%, we cut ours by 20. We were determined to *outdo* them.

- A *workshop* is a room or building containing work tools or equipment. Can you guess what these *work-* combinations mean?

  a workload
  a worksheet
  a workaholic

5 Approximate definitions

- Did you work out precise definitions for the words in italics in the article? For example,

  accent
  a pronunciation symbol, usually placed above a letter

  exchange rates
  the comparative value of different currencies

  drought
  a long period of time in which no rain falls

- Most of the time it is not necessary to define words so precisely. You just need a rough idea of what they mean. For example,

  wax
  something that makes shoes waterproof

  tin
  a sort of container

  lid
  a part of a container

- So don't worry if you are not 100% correct. The important thing is to read as much as possible. The more often you see an English word, the better you will understand it.

OBJECTIVE

to compare alternative
courses of action and
decide what to do

TASKS

to compare products
and make a purchasing
decision
•
to interpret statistics
and draw comparisons
•
to make business
choices involving
ethical issues
•
to discuss different
options for a company
visit
•
to consider alternative
ways of motivating
staff

PRESENTATION

1 Look at this form. What do you think it is for?

PRINT ESTIMATE

To: *Catherine Parker* Div: *Mailings* Date: *26 July*

Type: *4-colour catalogue* Extent: [ ] pages Quantity: *50,000*

FIXED COSTS

C41	Composition and proofs		9,200
A42	Corrections allowance @ _20_ %		1,840
I44	Litho origination		33,120
J46	Jacket/cover origination		400
	TOTAL FIXED COSTS		44,560
	per copy		0.89

VARIABLE COSTS

		Hong Kong	Europe
PP67	Paper, printing and binding	77,886	89,569
T70	Freight		
	TOTAL VARIABLE COSTS	81,386	90,569
	per copy	1.63	1.81

TOTAL PRODUCTION COSTS

	Hong Kong	Europe
per copy	125,946	135,129
	[ ]	[ ]

DELIVERY TIMES   [ ] weeks   [ ] weeks

RATE OF EXCHANGE   £1 = HK$ [ ]

2 🔲 Listen to two managers discussing price estimates. Complete the
missing information on the form.

3 🔲 Use words and phrases from the box to complete the sentences
below. Then listen again and check your answers.

| until   if   when   unless   in case |

1 _____ we order next week, when will they get here?
2 We ought to buy dollars now, _____ the rate changes.
3 I can't do that _____ I've got the go-ahead from head office.
4 I'll have a word with Finance _____ I see them.
5 Europe's *much* dearer, isn't it?
   Yes, _____ the Hong Kong dollar rises dramatically in the next
   few days.

Pronunciation

1 🔲 Listen to these phrases from the conversation again. Notice how some of the words are linked together.

1 But what about freight?

2 from Head Office

Notice that there is a vowel sound at the beginning of the second word.

2 Here are some more phrases from the conversation. Which words do you think are linked?

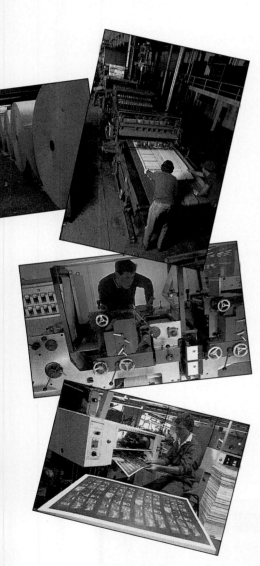

1 the same as last year

2 I'll have a word with ...

3 There's another factor.

4 I've calculated on the basis of ...

5 costs work out at two pounds thirty

🔲 Listen and see if you are right.

3 🔲 Sometimes we add an extra sound between two words when we link them together. Listen to these phrases from the conversation again. See if you can hear the short /w/ and /j/ sounds as in *wet* and *yet*.

1 the go   ahead
        /w/

2 I've got two   estimates.
              /w/

3 If we   order next week ...
     /j/

4 the   autumn catalogue
     /j/

Notice that there is a vowel sound at the end of the first word and the beginning of the second.

4 Here are some more sentences from the conversation. Which words do you think are linked?

1 I've used a rate of one pound to eleven Hong Kong dollars.

2 On the other hand, that's only a small part of the bill.

🔲 Listen and see if you are right. Then read the sentences aloud, paying attention to the linking sounds.

LANGUAGE WORK

Comparing products

1 You need to buy some cars for your company fleet and you are deciding whether to buy petrol- or diesel-powered models. First say whether you think these statements are true or false.

1 Diesel cars are generally cheaper to buy than petrol-driven cars.
2 Petrol-driven cars are more expensive to run than diesels.
3 Fewer people bought diesels in the past than now.
4 Over a car's lifetime, a diesel model will cost less money to run than a petrol-driven one.
5 The performance of petrol-driven cars is better.
6 Pollution from diesel cars is worse.

2 Now read the article and find out what the writer thinks.

The diesel route

In the past, diesel cars had a reputation for being noisier and more sluggish than their petrol-driven counterparts. But times have changed and more and more people are discovering that the modern diesel can match the performance of a petrol-driven model. Not only are diesels much more economical to run, but the exhaust from the latest diesel engines is as clean as that from a car with a catalytic converter running on lead-free petrol.

According to David Knight, managing director of PHH All-Star, Britain's largest fleet management company, the time has come for managers to change to diesel. 'They'll be unable to deny the benefits and financial savings of an all-diesel fleet,' he says. Data collected by PHH on the running costs of 120,000 company cars shows that petrol-engined cars used 37% more fuel than diesels, so over the lifetime of the vehicles the diesels worked out far cheaper.

Make	Model	Fuel	List price	Running cost pence per mile*	Diesel whole-life differential cost
Audi	100D 2.5	diesel	£23,211	32p	The diesel is £1,032.65 cheaper
Audi	100 2.6	petrol	£20,460	34p	
Citroën XM	Turbo 2.1	diesel	£23,035	34p	The diesel is £1,411.56 cheaper
Citroën XM	Turbo 2.0	petrol	£22,365	36p	
Rover	800 2.5	diesel	£18,595	29p	The diesel is £655.94 cheaper
Rover	800 2.0	petrol	£18,395	30p	

*PHH database figures calculated over 36 months/60,000 miles

3 Consider some of the different forms we use to make comparisons.

1 Look back at statements 1– 6 in Exercise 1 and underline all the comparative forms.
   a When do we use -*er* and when do we use *more*?
   b When do we say *fewer* and when do we say *less*?
   c What are the comparative forms of the adjectives *good* and *bad*?

2 We can't use *very* with comparatives.
   Diesels are ~~very~~ more economical.
   Look at the article and find two other words we use instead.

3 Look at the table. Which car is the most expensive to buy? Which car is the cheapest?
   When do we use comparative forms (*cheaper, more expensive*) and when do we use superlative forms (*the cheapest, the most expensive*)?

4 You are deciding between three different diesels for your company fleet. Work with a partner. Study this information from *What Car?* magazine and ask and answer questions about the cars.

Which car is the cheapest? And which is the most expensive?
Which car depreciates fastest?

Decide which car to buy.

Make and model	**Audi 100 TDI**	**Rover 825D**	**Citroën XM Turbo SED**
List price	£23,211	£18,595	£23,035
Length	187 inches	192 inches	185 inches
Width	79 inches	77 inches	79 inches
Height	56 inches	55 inches	55 inches
Boot	18 cubic feet	19 cubic feet	16 cubic feet
Tank	17.6 gallons	15.0 gallons	17.6 gallons
Maximum speed	124 mph	118 mph	116 mph
0-60 mph	10.2 seconds	11.8 seconds	10.3 seconds
Fuel consumption*	43.8 mpg	43.1 mpg	41.9 mpg
Retained value after 3 years **	38%	34%	26%
Cost per mile***	57.97p	53.56p	57.00p
What the price includes	♀ ♠ ➾ O ⊘ 🖫	♀ ⇦ ⊜ O ⊫ ⊘ 🖫 ♨	✿ ♀ ♠ ➾ ♩ O ⊘ 🖫 ♨
What Car?'s Verdict	Audi's likeable big saloon is unmatched as a diesel. Like all Audis, it's galvanised so will last.	Now with added kudos thanks to rounded lines. The 800 is dynamically average but feels very luxurious.	Striking-looking, wedge-shaped executive express that's good to drive and well equipped.

KEY mph = miles per hour, mpg = miles per gallon,	* = calculated travelling in towns for 50% of the time at constant speeds of 56 mph and 75 mph for the other 50% ** = Estimated % of original value retained after three years and 36,000 miles. *** = Calculated over 3 years and 36,000 miles. Includes fuel, depreciation and servicing.

KEY TO SYMBOLS ✿ air conditioning, ♀ central locking, ⇦ manual sunroof, ♠ electric sunroof, ➾ four electric windows, ♩ power seats, O electric mirrors, ⊘ seat height adj, ⊫ split/fold rear seats, 🖫 radio/cassette, ♨ steering height adj.

5 How do you think your car compares with these models? What factors were most important when you chose the car you drive?

Interpreting statistics

1 Find out about some other countries' standards of living. Look through these graphs with some colleagues. For each one

- see if your country appears on the graph. If so, how does it compare? If not, how do you think it would compare?

  The number of drug offences is about average.
  I think we have fewer violent deaths than they have in the US.

- comment on any interesting statistics you find.

  Sweden has the highest tax rates.
  Men live longer in Russia than in Saudi Arabia.

- explain the statistics wherever you can.

  People live longer in Japan because their diet is healthier.

> Unless marked otherwise, all graphs refer to the year 1988.

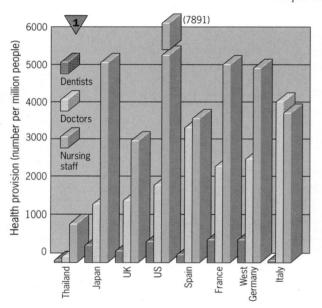

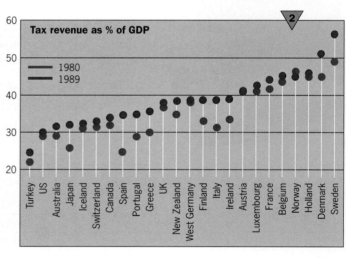

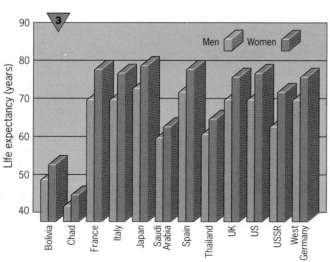

Consumer Goods (ranked by % households with each item)	Two TVs	Video	Phone	Home computer	Personal stereo	Microwave oven	Dish washer	Exercise machine	Car	Dog	Cat
West Germany	25	42	89	16	30	32	31	12	70	14	12
Italy	36	25	88	12	21	6	17	10	80	24	22
UK	36	58	85	22	35	49	12	15	63	25	21
France	23	35	85	14	36	24	33	8	75	31	24
Spain	35	40	65	8	18	9	10	5	62	18	12
Netherlands	31	48	95	20	32	19	10	7	69	20	23
Belgium	19	42	78	15	22	22	25	7	78	29	25
Portugal	20	22	51	7	12	4	11	3	46	29	18
Greece	16	37	74	6	16	2	10	0	46	15	13
Denmark	23	39	86	14	28	13	26	5	66	24	16

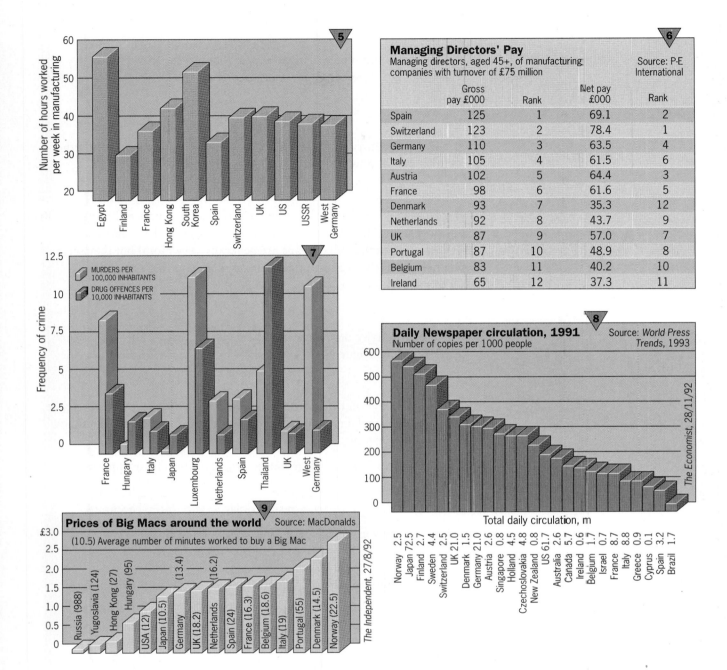

5 Number of hours worked per week in manufacturing

Egypt, Finland, France, Hong Kong, South Korea, Spain, Switzerland, UK, US, USSR, West Germany

6 Managing Directors' Pay
Managing directors, aged 45+, of manufacturing companies with turnover of £75 million

Source: P-E International

	Gross pay £000	Rank	Net pay £000	Rank
Spain	125	1	69.1	2
Switzerland	123	2	78.4	1
Germany	110	3	63.5	4
Italy	105	4	61.5	6
Austria	102	5	64.4	3
France	98	6	61.6	5
Denmark	93	7	35.3	12
Netherlands	92	8	43.7	9
UK	87	9	57.0	7
Portugal	87	10	48.9	8
Belgium	83	11	40.2	10
Ireland	65	12	37.3	11

7 Frequency of crime

MURDERS PER 100,000 INHABITANTS
DRUG OFFENCES PER 10,000 INHABITANTS

France, Hungary, Italy, Japan, Luxembourg, Netherlands, Spain, Thailand, UK, West Germany

8 Daily Newspaper circulation, 1991
Number of copies per 1000 people

Source: *World Press Trends*, 1993

The Economist, 28/11/92

Total daily circulation, m

Norway 2.5, Japan 72.5, Finland 2.7, Sweden 4.4, Switzerland 2.5, UK 21.0, Denmark 1.5, Germany 21.0, Austria 2.6, Singapore 0.8, Holland 4.5, Czechoslovakia 4.8, New Zealand 0.8, US 61.7, Australia 2.6, Canada 5.7, Ireland 0.6, Belgium 1.7, Israel 0.7, France 8.7, Italy 8.8, Greece 0.9, Cyprus 0.1, Spain 3.2, Brazil 1.7

9 Prices of Big Macs around the world   Source: MacDonalds

(10.5) Average number of minutes worked to buy a Big Mac

Russia (988), Yugoslavia (124), Hong Kong (27), Hungary (95), USA (12), Japan (10.5), Germany (13.4), UK (18.2), Netherlands (16.2), Spain (24), France (16.3), Belgium (18.6), Italy (19), Portugal (55), Denmark (14.5), Norway (22.5)

The Independent, 27/8/92

2   You are thinking of leaving your country and working abroad for a few years. Which countries would you like to move to? Which countries would you *not* like to move to? Explain your choices to your colleagues. You can refer to information from the graphs, and you might also like to refer to other factors such as

- the pace of life
- the climate
- the culture
- the nightlife
- the beauty of the countryside
- the difficulty of learning a new language
- schooling for your children.

Moral standards

1   Are some nationalities more honest than others? Do different countries have different moral standards? Read the article on the opposite page and find out.

2   Is your country on the chart? If so, how does it compare with other nations? If not, how do you think it might compare?

3   Generally speaking, each country's individual scores reflect its overall position quite closely. But some nationalities seem to have surprising vices. For example, Norwegians are generally very moral but they seem surprisingly likely to cheat on their taxes. Can you find any more surprising results?

4   Which activity on the chart is the most antisocial and which is the least? What punishments do you feel are appropriate for these activities?

5   The activities in the chart are all *antisocial*. *Anti* is a prefix. It can be put in front of *social* to form a word that describes activities that annoy or harm other people.

Add prefixes to these words from the article to form their opposites.

| .... justified | .... moral | .... honest |
| .... legal | .... responsible | .... accurate |

Think of more words that begin with these prefixes.

6   Which prefixes are used with these words to form their opposites?

.... fair	.... correct	.... possible
.... polite	.... regular	.... convenient
.... relevant	.... logical	.... reliable
.... organized	.... efficient	.... practical
.... likely	.... certain	.... probable

Civic Morality

I f you happen to drop your wallet in Europe, try not to drop it in Lisbon. It seems most Portuguese think it is sometimes or always justified to keep any money they find. Try to drop it in Belfast instead. Only a few people in Northern Ireland would consider keeping it, or so they say.

These insights into our vices come from a massive European study of civic morals. Nearly 19,000 individuals in 13 countries were surveyed by the European Value Systems Study Group, a network of academics across the continent. They listed ten antisocial and illegal activities, ranging from littering to tax evasion, and asked people how often they could be justified.

The results show that Europe's most moral and responsible citizens are the Danes, and the French are the least, but the researchers acknowledge that some nationalities may have been more honest than others when answering the questions. So how accurate are their findings? Perhaps the group's next survey should be on whether it's justifiable to lie to social scientists when they ask you questions.

	DENMARK	NORTHERN IRELAND	NORWAY	ICELAND	SWEDEN	BRITAIN	ITALY	THE NETHERLANDS	GERMANY	SPAIN	PORTUGAL	BELGIUM	FRANCE
Claiming State benefits you are not entitled to	2	5	1	7	4	6	8	3	9	12	11	10	13
Avoiding fares on public transport	2	3	1	8	5	6	4	7	9	10	13	11	12
Cheating on your tax returns	2	1	11	7	3	5	4	9	8	6	12	13	10
Buying goods that you know are stolen	1	2	3	5	4	8	6	7	10	9	11	12	13
Joy-riding	2	1	8	3	4	5	9	12	6	13	7	11	10
Keeping money you find	3	1	4	2	5	6	9	7	8	11	13	12	10
Accepting a bribe	1	3	4	2	7	6	8	10	11	5	9	13	12
Not reporting damage you did to a parked car	1	5	2	6	3	12	9	8	4	7	11	10	13
Dropping litter in the streets	1	12	7	6	13	11	2	9	10	4	3	8	5
Driving when you are drunk	1	3	4	8	2	5	6	7	12	9	10	13	11
OVERALL	1	2	3	4	5	6	7	8	9	10	11	12	13

SOURCE: The European, March 5 1992

The numbers in the table give the countries' overall moral position compared with other European countries. The final column gives their overall moral position as calculated by the European Value Systems Study Group.

Business ethics

How ethical are you in your business dealings? Find out with the questionnaire on the opposite page. Work with some colleagues. Keep a record of your answers to check your scores at the end.

Contingency plans

1   An important customer is visiting your place of work tomorrow and you are responsible for her visit.

What will you do if
1   she can't speak English?
2   she needs transport to your office from the airport?
3   you have to keep her waiting while you take an urgent call?
4   she'd like to try some local food for lunch?
5   it starts to rain as you begin your tour of the site?
6   her flight home is cancelled and she has to stay overnight?

If she can't speak English, I'll hire a translator.

2   *If* is a useful word for talking about future plans. But it isn't the only word we can use. Explain the difference in meaning between these pairs of sentences.

1   We'll hire an interpreter *if* she can't speak English.
    We'll hire an interpreter *in case* she can't speak English.

2   We could introduce her to the designer *if* he's free.
    We could introduce her to the designer *when* he's free.

3   He can show her the plans *if* he's changed them.
    He can show her the plans *unless* he's changed them.

4   She won't renew the contract *if* we alter it.
    She won't renew the contract *until* we alter it.

3   Now imagine you are talking to a visitor. Complete these sentences in your own words.

1   We're building some new workshops. I could show you round the building site if …
2   You'll be able to see what the workshops will be like when …
3   And you can meet the Project Leader unless …
4   Let's go. You can leave those papers in my office until …
5   But don't leave anything valuable in case …
6   It's best to go on foot unless …
7   Could you put this helmet on in case …
8   You can take it off again when …

1 You do a lot of travelling on business. Your company pays your air fares and you have collected 'frequent flyer' miles from the airlines that you can exchange for free flights. If you use them for your own personal travel, nobody will know. *Will you*

a use them for business trips and save your company money?
b use them to upgrade your seat to first class on business trips?
c book that holiday in the Bahamas that you've always wanted?

2 You are the manager of a charming pub in the country a long way from the nearest town. The owner of the pub wants you to run an 'all you can drink' campaign where the customers can have as much beer as they want for a fixed price. It's bound to attract more customers and be very profitable. *Will you*

a refuse to do it, in case it encourages people to drink and drive?
b agree to do it, but put up posters warning against drink-driving and start selling black coffee as well as beer?
c refuse to do it unless you receive a profit-related bonus?

3 You are the owner of a small business. One of your suppliers, an old friend, has asked you to pay them cash for an order so they can avoid paying VAT. There's no chance of your getting into trouble even if the tax office find out because it is your supplier's responsibility to declare it, not yours. *Will you*

a refuse?
b warn your friend that they could get into trouble but agree if they insist?
c agree? (After all, what are friends for?)

4 You have run out of stationery at home and there's plenty of nice blank paper and envelopes in your desk at work. *Will you*

a resist the temptation to take any home?
b take a little home to keep yourself going until you can buy some more?
c take plenty home so you don't run out again?

5 You work in the purchasing department of a large company. One of your suppliers has sent you a Christmas present—a case of wine. They know you shouldn't accept it because they also sent a note promising not to tell any of your colleagues about it. *Will you*

a send the wine back and never buy anything from that supplier again?
b send the wine back and explain you can only accept gifts up to a certain value?
c send the wine back and say that you prefer fine malt whisky?

6 You are a financial manager. Until last year, your company had an unbroken record of rising earnings per share, but last year's profits were down. Fortunately you have received a very large order since the beginning of the present financial year. Your boss tells you to record the new order in last year's accounts, so you don't spoil the company's track record. *Will you*

a explain it might mislead shareholders and refuse?
b refuse unless you can include a note about it in the small print in the annual report?
c agree and suggest some other 'legal' ways of making the figures look better this year?

7 You are friendly with someone in the strategic planning department of your company. One day, they give you some confidential information. They tell you about a company they are going to target for take-over. They are sure the share price will rise. You could make a lot of money if you buy shares now. *Will you*

a tell your colleague they shouldn't pass on confidential information?
b thank your colleague but do nothing?
c tell your broker to buy as many shares as they can?

8 You are the owner of a small company. A friend offers you a free copy of a computer software program that you need at work. If you accept their offer, you won't have to pay the $700 licensing fee to the software company. *Will you*

a turn down your friend's offer and buy your own copy?
b accept your friend's offer?
c accept their offer and charge the company $700 which you can pocket tax-free?

How did you score?

Mostly as

You may not always be popular with your colleagues but your business contacts know they can trust you to play fair. If some people accuse you of being inflexible, it's because your strong principles make them feel uncomfortable. Your honest approach should bring you success in your career and, although it may be slow coming, it's bound to be long-lasting.

Mostly bs

You like to do what's right if you can, but realize the world is not an honest place. You've probably noticed the person who tells the truth is not always the person who gets on fastest so you are prepared to make compromises, accepting the fact that in order to do business you sometimes have to bend the rules.

Mostly cs

If the people around you are behaving dishonestly, you will do everything necessary to ensure they don't get your share. As you see it, if you can't beat them, join them. No doubt you will advance up the ladder of success at top speed because you are very good at telling people exactly what they want to hear. The trouble is, it is not always what they *should* hear, so your success will probably be short-lived.

SKILLS WORK

Speaking   **1** Work in small groups. You are the managers of a company that is having difficulties with low motivation among its workforce. It's your job to tackle the problem.

Start by pooling your ideas in a brainstorming session. Think of different things that motivate people to work harder. Brainstorm as many different motivators as you can. For example,

higher pay
working in teams
opportunities for promotion.

One person in the group should write a list. Help them by expressing your ideas in short phrases.

2 Look at your list and select the most important motivators to add to the chart below. Then, working individually, rank them. Give 1 to the most effective, 2 to the second most effective, and so on. (Don't worry about the practicalities of introducing them at this stage. Just consider how effective you think they are.)

	Your ranking	Team ranking
Higher pay		
Working in teams		
Opportunities for promotion		

3 Now share your opinions with your group and work out a team ranking.

4 Some of these motivators will be easier to introduce into the work place than others; and some will be more expensive to introduce than others. For each one, discuss what problems you are likely to encounter and decide on the best way of overcoming them.

5 MORI, a consumer research company, conducted a survey into motivation. Compare your ideas with their survey results in File 10 on page 155.

Listening

1 Steve Coppell is one of the most distinguished managers in English football. For nine years he managed Crystal Palace football team, and during that time he succeeded in transforming them into a highly successful premier division side. You are going to hear his views on motivating a team. Before you listen, decide whether you agree with these statements.

1 Managers should encourage staff to spend time together outside work to develop a team spirit.
2 It's better to motivate workers as a team rather than trying to motivate them individually.
3 People perform better when they are relaxed than when they are under pressure.
4 Managers should select their team, tell them what they've got to do and then leave them alone to get on with it.
5 If a worker is demotivated, it's their manager's duty to try to re-motivate them.

2 Now listen and find out whether Steve Coppell would agree with the statements. Do his views differ from yours?

3 Listen again and complete these sentences.

1 When players choose to spend time together, ...
2 If they're too tense, ...
3 If they prove incompetent, ...
4 If I've chosen those eleven players to get a result, ...
5 If I'm dropping a player from the team, ...
6 If they want to discuss it, ...
7 If I have a player who is magnificently gifted but has a stinking attitude, ...

129

OBJECTIVE

to participate in
decision-making in
meetings

TASKS

to establish how
problems have arisen
and decide how to
deal with them

•

to check you
understand what's
been said at a meeting

•

to summarize the
views of other
participants

•

to justify and reject
proposals and collect
other people's
opinions

•

to hold a meeting to
decide on a business
strategy

PRESENTATION

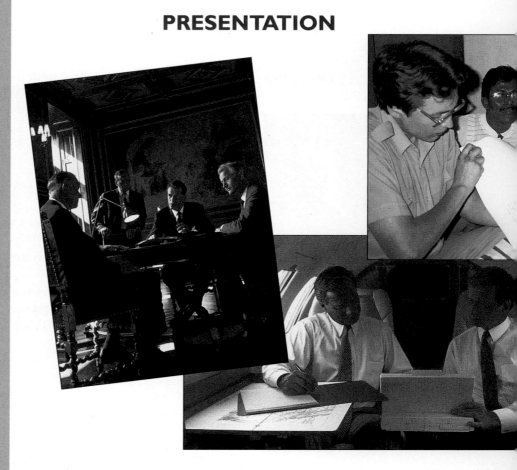

1 🔲 Three managers are holding a meeting to discuss a problem they
are facing. Listen to Part 1. Find out what the problem is and how it arose.

2 🔲 Listen again and note who did these things. Was it the designer
(D), the engineers (E), or both (D/E)?
Who
• changed the design?
• incorporated a smaller battery?
• moved a socket?
• couldn't meet the new specifications?
• built the prototype?
• didn't check that what they were doing was OK?

Complete this sentence in your own words.
If they had checked before they built the prototype, ...

3 🔲 Now listen to Part 2. The managers are discussing what to do next.
What two options do they consider?

4 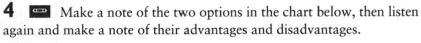 Make a note of the two options in the chart below, then listen again and make a note of their advantages and disadvantages.

Options	Advantages	Disadvantages
1		
2		

5 Use your notes to make sentences about the different options.
If they went back to stage one, they'd be able to meet all the specifications.

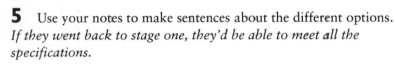

> **VOCABULARY NOTE**
>
> Do you know when to use the verbs *to say* and *to tell*?
>
> We often use *say* with the actual words spoken.
> *Are you saying we can't do it?*
> *She said 'Yes, of course.'*
>
> We often use *tell* if we are passing on information or giving instructions.
> *Could you tell us about the problem?*
> *I told them to check with me first.*
>
> In many situations we can use either *say* or *tell*.
> *They said it wasn't their fault.*
> *They told me it wasn't their fault.*
>
> But notice *tell* is followed by the person being told. *Say* isn't.
>
> These sentences are wrong.
> ~~*They told it wasn't their fault.*~~
> ~~*They said me it wasn't their fault.*~~

Pronunciation

Vowel sounds
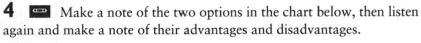 Listen to these words. In each group there is one word that has a different vowel sound to the rest. Which one is it?

1	meet	mean	it	be
2	change	say	said	rate
3	work	firm	heard	draw
4	fill	feel	will	built
5	they	check	debt	lend
6	sure	four	word	more

LANGUAGE WORK

Checking understanding

1 It's important to ask the right questions to make sure you understand what people are saying in meetings.

Supposing you were at a meeting and someone said
I think we should redesign the product.

Look at some of the different things you could say.
1 *Could you slow down?*
2 *Sorry. I don't follow.*
3 *What do you mean by 'redesign'?*
4 *What does 'redesign' mean?*
5 *Could you say it again more slowly?*
6 *Sorry. What was that?*
7 *Sorry. I'm not with you.*
8 *I didn't catch that.*
9 *You think we should what?*

Sort them into groups. Which ones would you say if
a you didn't hear what they said?
b they spoke too fast?
c you didn't understand anything?
d you don't understand the word 'redesign'?
e you don't understand what they mean by 'redesign'?

Compare your answers with some colleagues. Some expressions may fit into more than one group.

2 Practise the question forms with some colleagues. Take it in turns to give your opinions on one of the topics below. Your colleagues should interrupt, asking questions to check they understand.
- smoking in public places
- divorce
- increasing crime rates
- football hooligans
- racism
- privatization

3 When you are asking a question, it helps to be exact. Notice some of the phrases we use to ask very specific questions.

A *I think we should reduce our staffing costs.*
B **Do you mean** *we shouldn't replace staff who resign?*
C Or **are you saying** *we should cut wages?*
D Or **are you suggesting** *we should make staff redundant?*

Work with a partner. Think of some similar questions to ask about each of these proposals. Begin with the phrases in **bold type** in B – D above and invent your own endings.

1 We have to improve the staff's level of English.
2 I think we should improve the quality of our products.
3 We need to reduce our heating bills.
4 We ought to get larger discounts from our suppliers.
5 We must increase our market share.
6 We should employ fewer people at senior management level.

4   Summarizing is another way of checking you understand. In this exercise you will practise summarizing a colleague's views.

Select a topic from the list below. Think of one point in favour of the topic and one point against it.

- military service
- private schools
- working abroad
- open-plan offices
- space travel research
- jogging

Now work with a partner. Take it in turns to state your points. Your partner should listen carefully. When you have finished, they should give a brief summary of your views, checking they have understood correctly. Listen carefully and make sure their summary is 100% accurate.

Expressing opinions

I   Study these useful phrases for meetings. Which ones would you use to
a justify proposals?
b reject proposals?

☐ *It'd save money.*
☐ *It'd mean we could ...*
☐ *It'd be risky.*
☐ *It'd improve ...*
☐ *It wouldn't be cost effective.*

☐ *It wouldn't be right.*
☐ *It'd be very short-sighted.*
☐ *It'd enable us to ...*
☐ *It'd save time.*
☐ *It'd cause disputes.*

2   Work with a partner. Think of reasons for managers to justify or reject these proposals.

1 Reducing the training budget.
2 Banning smoking throughout the workplace.
3 Making building alterations to the workplace so disabled people can gain access.
4 Holding all meetings in English from now on.
5 Opening a crèche for employees' children.
6 Reducing the length of employees' tea and coffee breaks.

3   Here are some useful phrases for collecting other people's opinions.

What do you think, Kirsten?
Any reaction to that, Jean-Claude?
How do you feel about that, Jorge?
Do you have any views on this, Anna?
Peter?

Try using the phrases with one or two of your colleagues.

You are the directors of a small company that manufactures pet food. The recession has hit profits and you are looking for ways to cut costs and generate extra income.

You have each worked out different ways of finding some extra money. Explain your proposals, find out about your colleagues' proposals and then decide on the best course of action together.

If you are working in pairs, one person should use the proposals in File 14 on page 156, and the other should use the proposals in File 19 on page 158.

If you are working in threes, one person should use the proposals in File 2 on page 150, another should use the proposals in File 6 on page 152, and the other should use the proposals in File 21 on page 159.

Hypothesizing

1   What is the difference in meaning between these sentences?

1   *If we'd used cheaper ingredients, we'd have saved money.*
2   *If we used cheaper ingredients, we'd save money.*

Both the sentences are about hypothetical situations. Which one is referring to a future situation that is unlikely to happen? Which one is referring to a past situation that didn't happen?

Notice the tenses used in the two sentences. Can you name them?

2   Imagine what would happen in these hypothetical future situations. Complete the sentences.

1   If all employees owned shares in the company they worked for, ...
2   If there were more women in top management positions, ...
3   If the government gave more help to companies setting up operations in areas with high levels of unemployment, ...
4   If there were no state-run health service, ...
5   If I had to decide my company's employment policy on AIDS, ...
6   If the EC had one common currency, ...
7   If the West did more to help Russia and Eastern Europe, ...
8   If there was an international law against all trade in arms, ...

3   Now compare your endings with a colleague. Find out what they think would happen if the hypothetical situation *did* take place.

A   *What do you think would happen if all employees owned shares in the companies they worked for?*
B   *I think we'd see an increase in productivity because everyone would be more committed.*

4   Now hypothesize about these past situations. Imagine what you would have done if you had been better informed. For example,

You didn't know the airport was 15 kilometres from the city centre. You took a taxi.
If I'd known the airport was 15 kilometres from the city centre, I wouldn't have taken a taxi. I would have taken a train.

1   You didn't know it was a formal party. You went wearing jeans and a jumper.
2   Your client didn't give you her fax number. You had to post a letter to her instead.
3   Your customer was allergic to seafood. You took her to a fish restaurant.
4   Nobody told you the meeting was cancelled. You turned up.
5   You didn't know the company was in trouble. You bought their shares.
6   You thought you were allowed to park in front of the building. They towed your car away.
7   Your assistant didn't check the invoices before you paid them. You overpaid a supplier by $6000.
8   No one mentioned the fact that your client was a bad loser. You beat him at golf.

5   Have you had any lucky experiences in your life? Perhaps you were in the right place at the right time and something very fortunate happened. Hypothesize about what would or wouldn't have happened if you hadn't been so lucky.

SKILLS WORK

Reading   All managers make mistakes, but the good ones learn from them. Here are two managers' accounts of mistakes they made.

1   The stories are mixed up. Read the beginning of each one to find out what they are about. Then read the extracts quickly and decide if they are part of Lynda's story or Dick's. Write L or D against each extract.

MY BIGGEST MISTAKE

Lynda King Taylor

Lynda King Taylor, 41, is managing director of LKT Manpower Services. After studying behavioural sciences, she worked with the World Health Organization in India and Pakistan. She also trained under Fred Herzberg, the 1970s management guru, was an advisor to the Department of Employment and established her own consultancy in 1980.

❝ My biggest mistake was trying to save money on a lecture tour.

MY BIGGEST MISTAKE

Dick Beach

Dick Beach, 50, is manager of Dunkeld House Resort Hotel in Scotland. In the early sixties he spent several years running restaurants in Paris and Frankfurt before moving to Scotland and working his way up the hotel management ladder. Dunkeld House is part of the Stakis group and has a turnover of £3 million.

❝ My biggest mistake was doing too much talking and not enough listening.

a
It made me laugh at the time. Naturally, I apologized and refunded the money he had spent on the trousers. But in retrospect I realized I hadn't really interviewed him at all. I'd just talked *at* him.

b
Of course the worst happened. One of the flights was delayed and I missed all my connections. I didn't get to Singapore until midnight the next day and I was absolutely exhausted. And although I was in Singapore, my luggage was in Jakarta.

c
Of course I should have carried my suit and presentation tools in my hand-luggage. And I should have paid the extra for a direct flight. But I've learnt my lesson. These days, if I'm expected to be first class on arrival then I travel first class.

d
It was 1971 and I was manager of the Great Northern Hotel. One morning I was sitting in my office when someone turned up for an interview. We had advertised for a waiter so I was pleased to see a smart, good-looking fellow of about 23.

e
So my first mistake was not listening. I should have kept quiet and heard what he had to say. And my second mistake was assuming he was a waiter when he was nothing of the sort. I shouldn't have jumped to conclusions. Pity though. He could have been a good waiter.

f
I hadn't thought to take the business suit or the slides I needed for the presentation into the cabin with me. I was wearing a grubby old T-shirt and jeans. All the shops were shut and I had to appear on the platform at seven the next morning. What a nightmare!

2 The two stories have a similar structure. Put the extracts into the correct order. Use the table below.

	Lynda King Taylor	Dick Beach
The background		
An arrangement they made		
What happened as a result		
What they had to do		
What they should have done		

3 Make up your own short story to tell the class. Describe an experience you have had at work. It could be about

- a mistake you made yourself
- a mistake someone else made
- problems you encountered on a business trip
- something funny that happened in your workplace.

Don't forget to say what should and shouldn't have happened.

g

I sent him out to buy some trousers, gave him a jacket and told him to work in the restaurant. He was quite good, actually. But about three hours later I heard him shouting at my secretary 'Me no waiter'. Only then did we discover that he had actually come to be interviewed by one of our customers for a job as a cosmetics salesman.

h

There were plenty of scheduled flights, but I decided to look around for the cheapest fare. In fact I booked one which had six stops en route that cost about half the normal price.

i

During the interview I didn't learn very much about him apart from the fact that he had no experience and was from Iran. But he was keen to learn and I was short-staffed so I arranged for him to start immediately.

j

It was 1973 and I'd received an invitation to give a presentation to 500 top business people in Singapore. I was just starting out in business and my bank manager had made it clear that I had to keep my costs down.

GRAMMAR NOTE

Make **and** *do*

In some expressions we use the verb *make*.
> *We all make mistakes.*
> *My bank manager made it clear I had to keep my costs down.*

In others we use the verb *do*.
> *I wasn't sure what to do.*
> *I did too much talking and not enough listening.*

Make and *do* have similar meanings so it is often difficult to know which to use.

Make is often used for constructive or creative actions.
> *making suggestions*   *making plans*

Do is often used with unspecified actions or to talk about work.
> *Do something!*
> *Have you done the monthly figures yet?*

But be careful. These rules do not always apply and it's easy to make mistakes!

4   Decide whether we use *make* or *do* in front of these words and phrases.

.... an offer
.... a phone call
.... someone a favour
.... a complaint
.... a lot of damage
.... progress
.... research
.... a profit
.... an appointment
.... anything you like
.... an effort
.... your English homework
.... a decision
.... your best

5   Work with a colleague. Invent sentences or short conversations using the phrases above.

A *You loved your car, so why did you sell it?*
B *Someone made me an offer I couldn't refuse.*

Speaking   Your government is deregulating the air travel industry. You are considering the feasibility of launching a new airline, operating routes from your city to London, New York, and Australia. Hold a meeting to discuss your possible strategy.

1   What should your main objective be in this venture?
• To achieve a large market share?
• To develop a specialized niche in the market?
• Something else?

2   What sort of image would you want to create for your airline? Choose one or two of the following.
• Safe and dependable
• Low price
• Friendly and informal service
• Exotic and exciting
• Frequent flights
• Luxurious
• Attractive cabin staff
• Something else

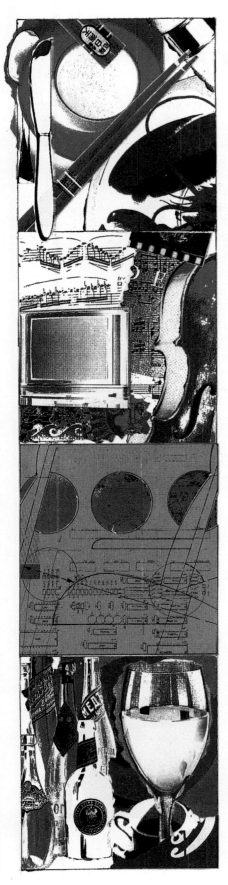

3 How many classes of travel should you offer?
- First class?
- Business class?
- Economy class?

4 Which of these services should you offer in each class?

	First	Business	Economy
• Food served on china plates			
• Four-course meals			
• Steel or silver cutlery (not plastic)			
• Plenty of leg-room			
• Plenty of space for hand-luggage			
• Complimentary drinks			
• On-board duty-free sales			
• A newspaper to read			
• A sweet to suck at take-off			
• Videos of the latest film releases			
• A relaxation audio tape for nervous flyers			
• Short waiting times between check-in and take-off			
• Hot flannels to freshen up with			
• Chauffeur-driven limousine to take travellers to and from the airport			
• Massages and manicures			

5 Should you provide any in-flight entertainment? (If so, what?)

6 Should you allow passengers to smoke?

7 You would like to give travellers a taste of your national identity when travelling. How could you do this?
- Cabin crew in national dress?
- Include national dishes in the menus? (What?)
- Play local music as passengers board and disembark?
- Feature your national identity in the decor? (How?)

Have you any other ideas?

8 What name would you give your airline?

9 What would your main problems be in this venture? How could you solve them?

OBJECTIVE

to make and follow
business presentations

TASKS

to follow a
presentation on
market research
findings

•

to outline the
structure of a talk

•

to make
recommendations to
clients or customers

•

to give a short talk on
a company issue

•

to report the results
of a market research
survey

•

to make a
presentation to a
client on a new
business venture

PRESENTATION

1 Work with a partner. Tell each other about the different sorts of newspapers you read. Are they

- daily or weekly papers?
- morning or evening papers?
- tabloids or broadsheets?
- national, regional, or local papers?
- papers you have to pay for or papers that are paid for by the advertisers?

In your opinion, which papers are

- the most informative?
- the most entertaining?
- the best medium for advertisers?

2 ▭ You are going to listen to a manager from a market research company making a presentation. Listen to her talk. What type of newspaper is most widely read, and what type does she recommend advertising in?

3 ▭ Look at the transparencies that Eva used in her talk. Listen again and fill in the missing statistics.

Which of these types of newspaper have you read in the last six months?

Base: 999 adults

Dailies
National tabloid	——%
National broadsheet	20%
Regional evening	26%
Regional morning	8%

Sunday newspapers
National tabloid	——%
National broadsheet	21%
Regional Sunday	6%

Weeklies
Regional paid-for	——%
Local paid-for	19%
Regional/local free	48%

None of these	4%
Don't know	1%

Source: BMRB/Mintel Market Intelligence

The consumer
Consumer characteristics for regional weekly paid-for newspapers

Base: 999

All 8%

Age group
15 – 19	
20 – 24	5%
25 – 34	6%
35 – 44	5%
45 – 54	8%
55 – 64	——%
65 +	8%
	7%

Socio–economic group
AB	——%
C1	7%
C2	9%
D	6%
E	3%

Source: BMRB/Mintel Market Intelligence

Tabloids and broadsheets

A news-vendor,
London, England

Buying a tabloid newspaper

4 ▣ Complete these sentences from the presentation. Use one word in each space then listen again and check your answers.

Part 1

Eva	Er ... how _____ time have we got?
Paul	Only a _____ , I'm afraid.
Eva	Well in that case, I'll begin straight away with a _____ of our survey results.
Roger	How _____ people did you question?
Eva	Just _____ a thousand.

Part 2

Paul	Do you _____ we advertise in the national tabloids?
Eva	No. I _____ you to advertise in the papers that attract the right sort of readers.
Eva	I _____ you concentrate your efforts on these weekly papers.

141

LANGUAGE WORK

Signposting talks

1 Presenters often signpost their talks to make them easier for the audience to follow. They explain what they will be talking about and when. Look at this introduction to a talk. Underline all the phrases that tell the audience how it will be structured.

'Good morning, ladies and gentlemen. As you can see from the conference programme, I'm going to be talking about franchising agreements. I'd like to begin by looking at franchising as a legal concept. Then I'll move on to franchising contracts with particular reference to royalty payments and start-up capital. If you have any questions, please feel free to interrupt, and I'll be happy to answer them as we go along.'

Can you think of any alternative phrases the speaker could use?

2 Now read a similar introduction. Underline the phrases that are different.

'Good afternoon, everyone. As you know, I'm here to tell you a little about franchising agreements. I'd like to start by considering franchising as a legal concept. Then I'll turn to franchising contracts: first looking at royalty payments, and then start-up capital. If you have any questions, I'll do my best to answer them at the end.'

3 Use these overhead transparencies to introduce some other presentations in a similar way.

Setting up facilities in Bavaria

1. The financial assistance available

2. Communications:
   • access to EC states and Western Europe
   • access to Eastern Europe

Preparing international air shipments

1. The importance of accurate labelling

2. Export documentation:
   • invoices
   • airway bills

---

4 Write similar notes showing the structure of a presentation you could give at work. Then use them to introduce the presentation.

Pronunciation

1 A speaker is preparing to read this text to an audience. Notice how they have divided it into small groups of words to show where they can pause if necessary.

'*Good morning ladies and gentlemen./As you can see/from the conference programme,/I'm going to be talking/about capital expenditure/in the Nestlé group./I'd like to begin by looking at/our plant modernization programme./Then I'll move on/to data-processing/and automation/with particular reference/to North America and Europe.*

Listen and notice how the speaker pauses very briefly at the end of each section.

2 If you have to read a text aloud, it can help to divide it into short sections. But you have to be careful where you pause. Is it possible to pause in these places?

'*Good/morning, ladies and gentlemen. As/you can see from the conference/programme I'm going/to be talking about capital/expenditure in the Nestlé group.*'

And what about these places?

'*I'd like to begin/by looking at our plant modernization programme./ Then/I'll move on to data-processing and automation/with particular reference to North America/and Europe.*'

There are no set rules about where you should pause, but you need to be logical.

3 Look at the introduction again. Which long words are difficult to pronounce? Mark where the main stress falls, e.g. *expenditure*

Listen again if necessary and check your answers.

4 Read another introduction to a presentation. This time there is no punctuation to help you see where one idea ends and another begins. Add punctuation, and mark where the speaker could pause.

'*good afternoon everyone as you know I'm here to tell you about British Telecom's video conferencing facilities I'd like to start by explaining how video conferences work then I'll turn to our facilities in the UK first our existing locations then the planned new ones*'

Now listen to the tape and see where the speaker pauses.

5 Mark where the main stress falls in the long words, then try reading the text aloud. Don't speak too fast, and remember to pause.

Making recommendations

1 Match the two halves of these sentences.

1 The wastage rate on this component is over 8%, so …

2 We expect the construction industry to suffer badly in this recession, so …

3 We are 100% certain we can win this case, so …

4 20% of your customers account for 80% of your sales, so …

5 Nearly a quarter of the calls your company receives come from abroad, so …

6 Only a few of the seats on this flight are allocated to business class passengers, so …

a we recommend your booking early.

b we recommend that you sell your shares in building companies.

c we advise you to take them to court.

d we advise targeting sales efforts at that group.

e we suggest you redesign it.

f we suggest classes in telephone English.

2 Who do you think gave this advice? Match each sentence above to one of these people.

- a travel agent
- a stockbroker
- a language trainer
- a lawyer
- a quality consultant
- a market research consultant

3 Look at the second halves of the sentences in Exercise 1. You can use several different word patterns after *recommend*, *advise*, and *suggest*, but be careful. Some word patterns are not possible. Look at these sentences. Find the patterns that are wrong, and cross them out.

1 We recommend booking early.
2 We advise to book now.
3 We advise against waiting.
4 We advise against to wait.
5 We suggest you book now.
6 We suggest you to book immediately.

4 Complete these recommendations then compare your answers with a partner.

1 That old machine is expensive to run, so we recommend …
2 A lot of cars have been stolen from around here, so I advise …
3 We're offering a special deal this month – up to 20% off, so I suggest …
4 If you'd like to try some local food, I recommend …
5 You can't afford to purchase three new vehicles outright, so I suggest …
6 He still owes me $50 from Christmas. So if he asks to borrow any money, I advise …

5   Who do you have to give advice to in your job? (Clients, customers, colleagues?) What subjects do you advise them on? What recommendations do you make?

Mini presentations

1   You are going to give a short presentation in English. What do you think will be most difficult?

1   Finding enough time to prepare?
2   Putting your points in order?
3   Speaking clearly — with good pronunciation?
4   Speaking accurately — with no mistakes?
5   Speaking fluently — without hesitating?
6   Handling questions from the audience?

2   Choose a subject for your presentation from this list.

Why my company is better than our competitors.
The biggest problem facing my company at the moment.
What my company must do to stay competitive in the future.

3   Now prepare what you are going to say. You can only speak for a few minutes so you must be brief.

1   What is your message? Write down the key point you want to get across. Use a maximum of ten words.
2   Now make notes on what you plan to say. Don't write sentences. Just write key words.

4   Give your presentation to some colleagues. They will listen very carefully and ask questions at the end.

Self-study task
Record your presentation onto a cassette and evaluate it. Give yourself a grade from A (excellent) to E (poor) for the following.
• Structure and organization
• Pronunciation
• Grammatical accuracy
• Fluency

Label and date the tape. It will be interesting to listen to it again in a few months to see if you have improved.

SKILLS WORK

Reading **1** How much have computers changed the way you work? Read these survey results and find out if you are typical.

MICROMYOPIA

An exclusive survey by Microsoft, the US software manufacturer, and *Management Today* magazine has revealed that although 76% of managers have direct use of screens and keyboards, only 6% believe they are used to maximum effect in their workplace.

One of the survey's most disturbing findings is that managers use computers to automate manual processes rather than to change work patterns and business practices. In most cases information technology (IT) is used to speed up routine tasks rather than as a competitive weapon.

Only a few use PCs on networks to share information and ideas. Instead, most managers use their PCs to edit documents — not a good use of their time when they could be dreaming up creative applications that will help them monitor their customers and competitors in a fast-changing marketplace.

What factors have stopped you using IT at work?

Had insufficient time to learn	58%
Received poor training/support	31%
Suffered from budgetary constraints	31%
Lacked keyboard skills	22%
Had poor systems	14%
Lacked interest	6%
Had no uses for it in my job	4%

Do you consider the IT in your organization is used to its full potential?

Yes, it's used to potential	6%
Adequate but some scope for improvement	42%
Considerable scope for improvement	49%
Don't know	3%

2 Use these phrases to make statements reporting the results of the survey.

Most	of the managers ...
Many	
Several	
A few	

Around	half	of the managers ...
Approximately	a third	
Nearly	a quarter	
Over		

3   What does the writer say about the way managers
- use computers?
- should use computers?

Do you agree?

> **GRAMMAR NOTE**
>
> English nouns can be divided into two groups: countable and uncountable.
>
> We use the words *many* and *a few* with countable nouns such as *computer* and *idea*. With uncountable nouns such as *information* and *help*, we use *much* and *a little*.

4   Complete this questionnaire about computers and IT (information technology). Use *much* or *many* in the spaces.

1. How _____ times have you used a computer in the last seven days?

2. How _____ time do you spend each day working on a computer?

3. How _____ staff have direct access to a computer in your work place?

4. How _____ has been spent on IT by your organization in the last two years?

5. How _____ of your organization's equipment needs updating?

6. How _____ of your work do you do on a computer?

7. How _____ effect have computers had on the way you work?

8. How _____ different software programs do you use on a regular basis?

9. How _____ training have you received in using IT?

10. How _____ help is available when you encounter difficulties?

5   Now ask and answer the questions with a colleague. Remember you can use *much*, *many*, *a little*, and *a few* in your answers too. You can also use *a lot*, with both countable and uncountable nouns.

Quite a	lot
	few
Only a	few
	little
Not	a lot
	much
	many

Speaking

Breaking into a market

Work in groups of three or four.

You are consultants to an American soft drinks company. They are planning to introduce a fizzy fruit drink into your home market. It is already successful in the US, where it is marketed as a healthy energy replacement for sports people. The company are employing you as consultants to help them position the product in the market. You have done some market research and now you are going to present your findings.

1 Study your survey results. What comments can you make about them in your presentation?

Why do you buy sports drinks?

Base: 1,500 adults

I like the taste.	52%
They give me energy.	49%
They satisfy my thirst.	42%
They are a natural product.	25%
They are good value for money.	19%
They help me to lose weight.	17%

The consumer

Percentage of adults who buy sports drinks.

Base: 1,500 adults

Men   31%
Women 19%

Age group		
	14 – 17	68%
	18 – 22	45%
	23 – 32	28%
	33 – 42	17%
	43 – 52	6%
	53 – 64	3%
	65 +	–%

Socio–economic group*		
	AB	21%
	C1	30%
	C2	39%
	D	52%
	E	29%

* People grouped according to income, education, and class. So, ABs would generally be well educated and earning high incomes; Es would generally be poorly educated and earning low incomes; Cs would be in the middle range.

2 Now discuss what recommendations to make to your client. You need to decide on

- the image of the product
- the name of the product
- a sports personality to promote it
- its price
- its container (can, carton, plastic bottle, glass bottle)
- the most suitable retail outlets (supermarkets, health food shops, chemists, street vending machines, sports centres)
- advertising (magazines, newspapers, direct mail shots, billboards, television, cinemas).

3 Plan how you will structure your presentation. You can follow the plan below or create your own. Decide which member of your group will present each section.
- An introduction, explaining the structure of the presentation
- The survey results
- The consumer profile
- Your recommendations
- Questions from the audience

4 Now give your presentation to the class and answer questions from the floor.

Role-play Notes

FILE 1 (see page 23)

1 You are the Sales Director of the UK subsidiary of a multinational company. Someone from your international headquarters phones you. You should do everything you can to help them. Use your diary.

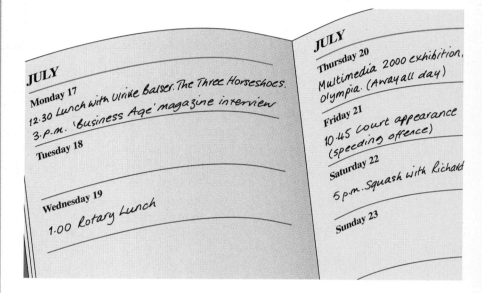

JULY

Monday 17
12.30 Lunch with Ulrike Balser. The Three Horseshoes.
3.p.m. 'Business Age' magazine interview

Tuesday 18

Wednesday 19
1.00 Rotary Lunch

JULY

Thursday 20
Multimedia 2000 exhibition. Olympia. (Away all day)

Friday 21
10.45 Court appearance (speeding offence)

Saturday 22
5 p.m. Squash with Richard

Sunday 23

2 It's now ten minutes later. Something has come up and you need to change the arrangement you just made. Phone your partner, explain what's happened (you'd better have a good excuse ready) and fix another time.

FILE 2 (see page 134)

Put these proposals forward at the meeting. Explain what they involve, why you think they are a good idea and then collect your colleagues' opinions.

Estimated saving/income	£
Put cheaper ingredients in the products	580,000
Freeze wages	342,000
Delay payments to our suppliers	60,000
Put one armed bandits in the staff rest rooms	18,000
TOTAL	**1,000,000**

Listen carefully to your colleagues' proposals and decide together which ones to accept and reject. You need to find at least £2 million.

FILE 3 (see page 23)

Your partner's country is hosting your company's annual international sales conference this year. They will phone you at head office to arrange the programme for the presentations. You have found out how many delegates are hoping to attend each one. Tell your partner and complete the programme.

Speakers	No. of Delegates	
Mr Tanaka	107	
Dr Joeckel (Germany)	56	Has to leave at 1.30pm
Ms Bocage (France)	72	Not arriving until lunchtime
Mr Alatali (Turkey)	28	Needs translation facilities
Ms Kirmanen (Finland)	28	Would like to speak before lunch
Mr Lucerni (Italy)	22	
Ms Morey (USA)	24	Needs video projection equipment

Programme	Session 1 (9.00-10.30)	Session 2 (11.00-12.30)	Session 3 (2.00-3.30)
Auditorium	Mr Tanaka		
Conference Room			
Meetings Room			

FILE 4 (see page 69)

Call 1   You are the editor of a trade magazine. One of your readers calls you about some mistakes in one of your articles. Make a note of the errors so you can print corrections along with an apology next month.

Call 2   A publisher has included an entry on you in an international directory of famous business people. Unfortunately, it contains a lot of mistakes. Phone the publisher to correct them.
1 They misspelt your name.
2 They said you are ten years older than you really are.
3 They misspelt the name of the school you attended.
4 They said you speak Chinese. (You don't.)
5 They misspelt your husband's/wife's name.

FILE 5   (see page 27)

1   Your partner has some information on Robert Bosch GmbH. Ask questions about

- the company's main business activities
- the location of the company's headquarters
- the company's total sales and gross margin
- the number of employees
- the company's current activities.

2   Now use the information on Komatsu to answer your partner's questions.

KOMATSU					
Principal business activities	**Head office**	**Turnover**	**Profit**	**Number of employees**	**Current projects**
The manufacture of construction equipment and industrial machinery.	Tokyo, Japan	$37,285m	$2,735m	23,817	Exploring business opportunities in the visual sensor and software development markets. Developing a new Computer Integrated Manufacturing system (CIM) to improve operating efficiency and enhance inter-company communications.

3   When you have finished, ask similar questions to find out more about your partner's own company.

FILE 6   (see page 134)

Put these proposals forward at the meeting. Explain what they involve, why you think they are a good idea and then collect your colleagues' opinions.

Estimated saving/income	£
Halve the research and development budget	600,000
Pack the products in paper cartons instead of tins	350,000
Reduce the temperature in the offices to 18°C	34,000
Cancel the staff Christmas party	16,000
TOTAL	**1,000,000**

Listen carefully to your colleagues' proposals and decide together which ones to accept and reject. You need to find at least £2 million.

FILE 7 (see page 72)

You need to order some computer goods and you've heard that you can get the best deal at MacWarehouse. Phone the company and place the order. Check the prices as you only have an old catalogue. Ask about their payment terms.

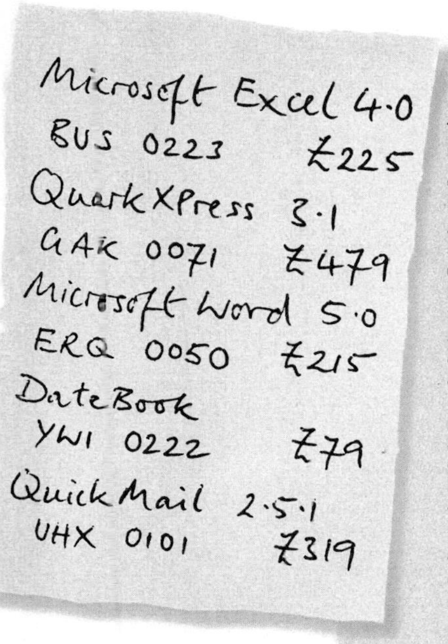

Handwritten note:

Microsoft Excel 4.0
BUS 0223   £225
QuarkXPress 3.1
GAK 0071   £479
Microsoft Word 5.0
ERQ 0050   £215
DateBook
YWI 0222   £79
QuickMail 2.5.1
UHX 0101   £319

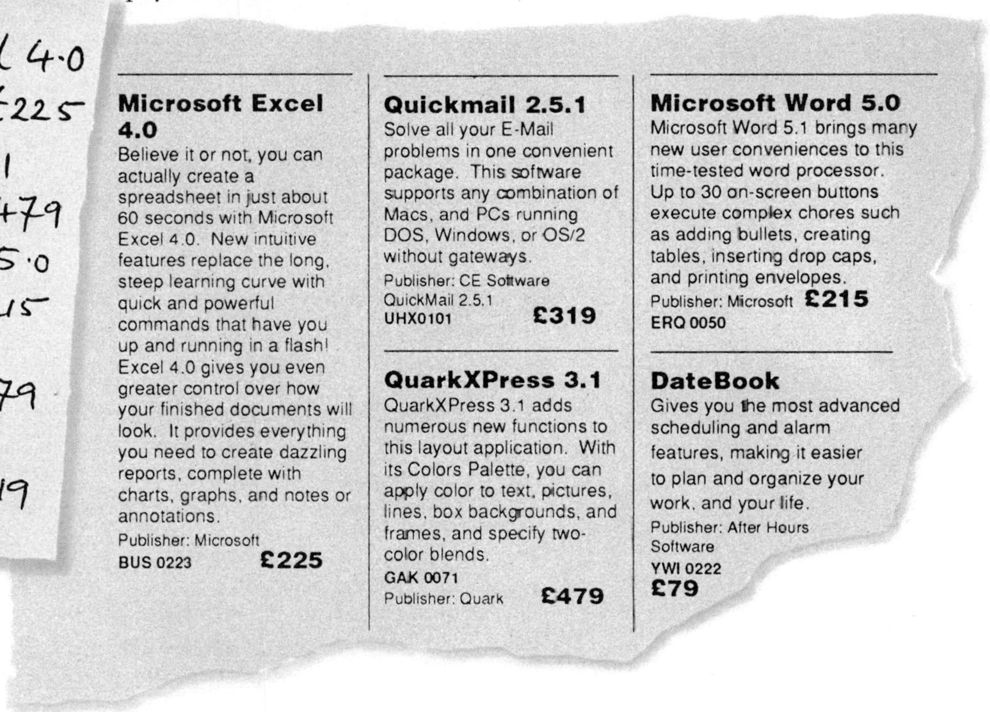

Microsoft Excel 4.0
Believe it or not, you can actually create a spreadsheet in just about 60 seconds with Microsoft Excel 4.0. New intuitive features replace the long, steep learning curve with quick and powerful commands that have you up and running in a flash! Excel 4.0 gives you even greater control over how your finished documents will look. It provides everything you need to create dazzling reports, complete with charts, graphs, and notes or annotations.
Publisher: Microsoft
BUS 0223   **£225**

Quickmail 2.5.1
Solve all your E-Mail problems in one convenient package. This software supports any combination of Macs, and PCs running DOS, Windows, or OS/2 without gateways.
Publisher: CE Software
QuickMail 2.5.1
UHX0101   **£319**

QuarkXPress 3.1
QuarkXPress 3.1 adds numerous new functions to this layout application. With its Colors Palette, you can apply color to text, pictures, lines, box backgrounds, and frames, and specify two-color blends.
GAK 0071
Publisher: Quark   **£479**

Microsoft Word 5.0
Microsoft Word 5.1 brings many new user conveniences to this time-tested word processor. Up to 30 on-screen buttons execute complex chores such as adding bullets, creating tables, inserting drop caps, and printing envelopes.
Publisher: Microsoft   **£215**
ERQ 0050

DateBook
Gives you the most advanced scheduling and alarm features, making it easier to plan and organize your work, and your life.
Publisher: After Hours Software
YWI 0222
£79

FILE 8 (see page 70)

1 **Karoshi:** Death which is caused by overwork.
2 **Namaste:** A greeting where you put your palms together and bow.
3 **Sköl:** Something people say to each other when they are having an alcoholic drink.
4 **Mafioso:** Someone who belongs to a secret criminal organization.
5 **Ramadan:** A month of the year when Muslims fast between sunrise and sunset.
6 **Fung shui:** Wind and water spirits which must be kept happy when a new building is erected.
7 **Kamaki:** A national 'sport' where young men pick up female tourists.
8 **Fasching:** A festival time when people wear funny clothes to work and visit beer gardens in the evening.
9 **Mall:** A covered area or building where there are many shops.
10 **Shadchan:** A person who arranges marriages.
11 **Ombudsman:** A person whose job it is to investigate complaints made by individuals about government authorities.
12 **Bortsch:** A soup that's made from beetroot and cabbage.

FILE 9   (see page 69)

DOCUMENTS

Here is a list of verbs that we frequently use with the documents.

You can	ask for prepare give	a quotation.

And of course, you can quote a price.

Quote is the verb (action) and *quotation* is the noun (thing) but *quote* can also be used as a noun, as a short form for *quotation*.

You can	place confirm acknowledge cancel	an order.

You can	check	a delivery note.

You can	issue query pay	an invoice. an invoice. an invoice.

You can	ignore	a reminder.

You can	write sign postdate endorse pay in	a cheque. a cheque. a cheque. a cheque. a cheque.
	put a cheque in the post.	

And if there aren't enough funds in the account, the bank will bounce the cheque!

You can	ask for issue lose	a receipt. a receipt. a receipt.

 FILE 10   (see page 129)

Look through the survey results below.

1 Do they include any of the motivators you discussed?

2 Do any of the findings support or contradict your opinions?

Which two or three of these would be most likely to encourage you to work harder at your job?

What motivates you to work harder?	
Greater financial reward	41%
A greater sense of 'team spirit' at work	26%
Working with people who work hard	23%
The chance of promotion	22%
Getting more encouragement from your boss	20%
Feeling that you, as an individual, are making a valuable contribution to your organization	19%
Feeling that you are making a valuable contribution to society	18%
Having a boss who works hard	17%
Working for a successful company	17%
Being given more responsibility	16%
Having a more challenging job	16%
Having a greater sense of belonging to the organization you work for	12%
Being self-employed	11%
A stronger sense of working for your country	9%
None of these	3%

Base: 2000
Source: MORI. Research study conducted for National Motivation Week.

 FILE 11   (see page 80)

CULTURE A

You come from a culture where people pause for a long time before they speak, taking time to think about what they are going to say. And when they do speak, they speak very slowly. You must behave in this way at the conference, BUT DON'T TELL ANYONE WHAT YOU ARE DOING.

Observe the other people at the conference closely. Do you notice anything unusual about their behaviour? What sort of culture do you think they come from?

FILE 12   (see page 48)

Jan Ludwig Hoch is better known as Ian Robert Maxwell, the media magnate. He died in mysterious circumstances in 1991 when his body was found floating in the Atlantic Ocean. Many people believe that he had a heart attack and fell off the side of his yacht but this theory is open to doubt. He was buried on the Mount of Olives in Israel. A few weeks after his death it was discovered that over £300 million was missing from the pension funds of *The Mirror Group* .

FILE 13   (see page 67)

PRONUNCIATION OF THE ALPHABET

Sound 1	Sound 2	Sound 3	Sound 4	Sound 5	Sound 6	Sound 7
/eɪ/	/iː/	/e/	/aɪ/	/əʊ/	/uː/	/ɑː/
as in *page*	as in *see*	as in *ten*	*five*	*home*	*you*	*arm*
A	B	F	I	O	Q	R
H	C	L	Y		U	
J	D	M			W	
K	E	N				
	G	S				
	P	X				
	T	Z (British English)				
	V					
	Z (US English)					

FILE 14   (see page 134)

Put these proposals forward at the meeting. Explain what they involve, why you think they are a good idea and then collect your partner's opinion.

Estimated saving/income	£
Halve the research and development budget	400,000
Pack the products in paper cartons instead of tins	270,000
Freeze wages	244,000
Delay payments to our suppliers	50,000
Reduce the temperature in the offices to 18°C	18,000
Put one-armed bandits in the staff rest rooms	18,000
TOTAL	**1,000,000**

Listen carefully to your partner's proposals and decide together which ones to accept and reject. You need to find at least £1,500,000 in total.

FILE 15 (see page 80)

CULTURE B

You come from a culture where people use their hands a lot when they are speaking. They also speak very loudly to show they are interested. You must behave in this way at the conference, BUT DON'T TELL ANYONE WHAT YOU ARE DOING.

Observe the other people at the conference closely. Do you notice anything unusual about their behaviour? What sort of culture do you think they come from?

FILE 16 (see page 71)

There are no clues to this crossword, but you have half the answers and your partner has the other half so you need to explain the words to each other. You can say anything you like to help your partner, but of course, you mustn't say the missing words.

FILE 17 (see page 80)

CULTURE F

You come from a culture where people speak very fast. They also like to stand a long way away from the person they are talking to. You must behave in this way at the conference, BUT DON'T TELL ANYONE WHAT YOU ARE DOING.

Observe the other people at the conference closely. Do you notice anything unusual about their behaviour? What sort of culture do you think they come from?

FILE 18 (see page 80)

CULTURE C

You come from a culture where it is rude to look people in the eye when you are listening or speaking, so you try to avoid eye contact as much as possible. You must behave in this way at the conference, BUT DON'T TELL ANYONE WHAT YOU ARE DOING.

Observe the other people at the conference closely. Do you notice anything unusual about their behaviour? What sort of culture do you think they come from?

FILE 19 (see page 134)

Put these proposals forward at the meeting. Explain what they involve, why you think they are a good idea and then collect your partner's opinion.

Estimated saving/income	£
Stop all spending on advertising	480,000
Put cheaper ingredients in the products	358,000
Demand larger discounts from our suppliers	60,000
Travel economy class instead of first class on flights	50,000
Install meters in the staff car park	36,000
Cancel the staff Christmas party	16,000
TOTAL	**1,000,000**

Listen carefully to your partner's proposals and decide together which ones to accept and reject. You need to find at least £1,500,000 in total.

FILE 20 (see page 80)

CULTURE E

You come from a culture where people don't move their hands, faces, or bodies when they are speaking. They also speak very quietly. You must behave in this way at the conference, BUT DON'T TELL ANYONE WHAT YOU ARE DOING.

Observe the other people at the conference closely. Do you notice anything unusual about their behaviour? What sort of culture do you think they come from?

FILE 21 (see page 134)

Put these proposals forward at the meeting. Explain what they involve, why you think they are a good idea and then collect your colleagues' opinions.

Estimated saving/income	£
Stop all spending on advertising	754,000
Demand larger discounts from our suppliers	150,000
Travel economy class instead of first class on flights	60,000
Install meters in the staff car park	36,000
TOTAL	**1,000,000**

Listen carefully to your colleagues' proposals and decide together which ones to accept and reject. You need to find at least £2 million.

FILE 22 (see page 80)

CULTURE D

You come from a culture where people like to stand very close to one another. They also like to touch each other a lot. You must behave in this way at the conference, BUT DON'T TELL ANYONE WHAT YOU ARE DOING.

Observe the other people at the conference closely. Do you notice anything unusual about their behaviour? What sort of culture do you think they come from?

Tapescript

1 Jobs and Responsibilities

PRESENTATION

Conversation 1

A Mr Jensen?
B Yeah?
A Hello. I'm Josephine Marca from Renault.
B Hi. Nice to meet you.
A And you.
B It's good of you to come and get me.
A Not at all.
B Have you been waiting long?
A No, just a few minutes. How was the flight?
B It was fine thanks.
A Good.
B So where to now?
A Well, the meeting starts at three so I intend to take you to your hotel first.
B Great!
A May I help with your baggage?
B No, I can manage, thanks.
A We're going to take a taxi, so if we make our way to the exit ...
B Is the hotel far from here?
A No, just a twenty-minute ride.

Conversation 2

A If you follow me, the projection room is in here. Ah, Dieter. Sorry to disturb you.
B No problem.
A We're looking for Bernd. Have you seen him?
B No. I'm waiting for him too.
A Have you met Signora D'Amore?
B No, I haven't.
A Then let me introduce you. Signora D'Amore, this is Dieter Nittel, our Sound Technician.
C How do you do?
B Pleased to meet you.
A Mrs D'Amore is from the Italian press office.
B Oh yes?
C We plan to install a video suite in Milan and I'd like to see the set-up here.
B Well, Herr Wick's the man to speak to. I'm sure he'll be happy to show you round when he gets back.
A Will he be long, do you think?
B I hope not.

Conversation 3

A Hello Ulla.
B Juan Carlos! Nice to see you. Do you know Mr Shingu?
A Yes. We met at last year's conference in Vancouver.
C Yes, and this time we're in your home town, aren't we?
A That's right. I live here in Alicante. What a good memory you've got.
B It's a beautiful city. We're just sorry we have no time to see round.
A That's a pity. When are you flying back?
B This evening.
A And you, Mr Shingu?
C I'm leaving tomorrow morning.
A What a shame. If you had more time, I'd take you sightseeing.
B I hope to come back soon, actually.
A Really? When's that?
B We haven't fixed the date yet but ...

LISTENING

A OK. Let's look at the new organization of Schering, France. Can everybody see that?
B Yes.
C Yes, it's fine.
A At the top here we have the General Manager and he has six people who report to him. There's the Director responsible for strategic co-ordination. Then there's me. I'm responsible for development and marketing. Then there's the Production Director, the Financial Director, the Personnel Manager and the Pharmaceutical Director. Any questions so far?
C No, none.
B It's very similar to the Nordic countries.
A OK. Let's look at my team in more detail then. As you can see, I have a Commercial Director, a Medical Director and then there are three Unit Directors. Two of them are responsible for domestic sales and one for foreign sales. But the interesting thing about these units is the work groups. As you can see, one unit has three work groups and another has four.
B That is rather different.
C What's the point of having these groups?
A They have a lot of advantages.

Firstly, each one works in a different medical field so they can develop the necessary specialized knowledge. Secondly, it's very motivating for the staff. Each group is a separate profit centre. They are totally in control of their own budgets so they have a lot of responsibility.

B How big are the groups?
A There are six people in each one. There's someone from marketing and someone from manufacturing. Then there are two doctors, one responsible for medical communication and the other working on research and development. There's someone from the sales force and someone from the Pharmaceutical Department. So each person represents a different section of our organization. And that's another big advantage. There's a wide range of expertise to draw on when they're making decisions.
C Yes, I see what you mean.
B It's very interesting indeed.

PRONUNCIATION

1 general
2 director
3 production
4 personnel
5 responsible
6 advantages
7 motivating
8 responsibility
9 development
10 expertise

2 Telephoning to make arrangements

PRESENTATION

Conversation 1

A Powerglide Systems.
B I'd like to speak to Emma Wood, please.
A Who's calling, please?
B Ernesto Garrone.
A One moment. I'll put you through.
C Emma Wood.
B Good morning. This is Ernesto Garrone.
C Hello, Mr Garrone. Nice to hear from you. How are you?
B Fine thanks, and you?
C Fine.
B I'm phoning about my visit on the 22nd. I'm afraid I've had to change my flight and I'm not arriving until eleven.
C Oh, right. Thank you for letting us know.
B And there's something else.
C Yes?
B Would you mind if I brought a colleague with me?
C Of course not. Can I have his name?
B Yes, it's a woman actually. Signora Agnelli, that's A-G-N-E-double L-I.
C Signora Agnelli.
B That's right. She'd like to have a look at your rolling mill.
C Would you like me to arrange a demonstration?
B That would be very kind.
C Not at all. Was there anything else?
B No, that's everything, I think.
C Let me know if there's anything else we can do.
B Thank you.
C Until Thursday at around eleven, then.
B Yes, I'm looking forward to meeting everyone.
C Thank you for calling. Goodbye.

Conversation 2

A Emma Wood.
B Ah Emma. It's Kjell Olaffsson here.
A Hello Kjell. What can I do for you?
B It's this visit by Ernesto Garrone.
A Yes?
B I'm afraid I can't make lunch on Thursday.
A That's a pity.
B Louise can, so it's not a major problem, but I was looking forward to seeing him. Could we meet on Friday instead?
A He's going to the Peterborough plant.
B I know, but how about a breakfast meeting?
A Yes, that would be possible.
B Shall we say 8.30 at the Dorchester?
A Yes, OK. And a colleague is coming with him.
B Is that Signora Agnelli?

A Yes.
B Fine. Would you put it on the schedule, then?
A Yep. No problem.
B Thanks a lot, then. Bye.
A Bye.

Conversation 3

A Michael Black.
B Hello Michael. Emma here.
A Hello Emma. I got the schedule.
B Good. The reason I'm calling is there have been some changes.
A Oh yes?
B Mr Garrone is bringing a colleague — a Mrs Agnelli. Would you mind showing her the rolling mill in operation?
A No, not at all.
B That's very good of you.
A When would suit you best?
B Some time on Thursday, if possible. Would you prefer the morning or the afternoon?
A The afternoon, I think. What about two o'clock?
B That should be fine. We were going on a workshop tour at 2.30 but I can put that off till three.
A Right then.
B So that's two on Thursday, then. Thanks a lot, Michael.
A You're welcome. Take care.
B And you. Bye.

LISTENING

A Could we have a quick word about the sales conference?
B Yes, of course. The venue's booked.
A Good. And I've got some definite numbers now. There are 107 delegates.
B That's OK. The auditorium holds 130, and I've booked two other rooms as well.
A We need to sort out the programme.
B It's difficult to do that without knowing how many people are attending each talk. There's a conference room that holds 60 people and a meetings room that holds 30.
A Well, everyone's going to Mr Tanaka's presentation. He's giving the opening address. But I'll find out about the others.
B Would you also ask the speakers if

they need any special equipment?
A What have you got, then?
B There are simultaneous translation facilities in the auditorium and there's a video projector in the conference room.
A What about microphones and slide projectors?
B All the rooms have them.
A Good.
B What time would you like to start?
A Nine, I think, then we can fit two sessions in before lunch. What are we doing for lunch?
B There's a bar for drinks and I thought we'd have a buffet.
A Don't they do sit-down meals?
B Yes. Would you prefer a sit-down meal, then?
A I think so.
B OK, I'll arrange it.
A And I'll find out how many people are going to each presentation.
B And what equipment the speakers need.
A Yes. OK.

3 Organizations

PRESENTATION

L'Oréal is active in all world markets and we employ just over thirty thousand people worldwide. We have production facilities, agents and subsidiaries in all five continents and we are increasing our share of the world's cosmetics markets.

Let's begin by looking at the different activities of the group. This slide shows last year's sales when we had a turnover of thirty-seven point five seven billion French francs. If we look more closely we can see that the largest part of our revenue comes from Consumer and Salons activities. This market segment accounts for forty-nine per cent of the total turnover. It includes skincare products, make up, fragrances and hair care products where we are a world leader.

The next division is perfumes and beauty. Here we have an exceptional range of prestigious brands which includes Lancôme, Helena Rubenstein and Biotherm. This division's turnover increased last year to stand at eight-and-a-half billion francs.

Moving on to Active Cosmetics, this division has dual objectives; firstly to develop new, technically advanced cosmetics and secondly to enhance our

close relationships with pharmacists — a key channel of distribution. It achieved a turnover of three point seven billion French francs last year.

Then we come to Synthelabo, our pharmaceutical subsidiary, which accounts for sixteen point eight per cent of our total revenues. It regularly invests twenty per cent of its turnover in research and development. Synthelabo is making advances in the treatment of central nervous system disorders at the moment, and it will become a world leader in this field in the future.

In addition to these four major areas of activity, L'Oréal also owns Artcurial, a contemporary art gallery, we hold a major stake in the Marie-Claire publishing group and we have increased our stake in Paravision International, a film production and distribution company. Together these activities account for one point eight per cent of our turnover, or nought point seven billion francs.

PRONUNCIATION

1 A Could you give me his phone number?
   B Yes, it's oh eight six five, two six seven, six double two.

2 C How many people were at the meeting?
   D Sixteen.

3 E We've gotten sixty enquiries so far.
   F Good. And how many have you replied to?
   E About two-thirds.

4 G How many kilometres are there in a mile?
   H One point six.

5 I Brrr. It's freezing today.
   J Yes, it's minus eight degrees out there.

6 K When were you born?
   L Nineteen fifty-eight.
   K Were you? I was born in fifty-nine.

7 M What's the population of Sweden?
   N Around eight and a half million.

8 O I'm free on the Friday of that week.
   P OK. That's the eighteenth of July, then.

9 Q My flight leaves at 16.50.
   R Then we'd better leave for the airport at about half past two.

10 S How much did it cost?
    T Nine hundred and ninety-nine dollars and ninety-nine cents.

4 Planning Ahead

PRESENTATION

A Bob Shaw.
B Hello, Bob. This is Victoire. I'm just phoning about your presentation next week. I think we should check everything again.
A Again?
B It's a big contract, Bob. I don't think we should take any chances.
A There is one thing, actually. I've got the address but I'm not sure where the office is.
B Aren't you going to take a taxi?
A No. I'm hiring a car.
B Then I'll fax you a map with directions.
A Thanks.
B Are you going to use an overhead projector?
A Yes.
B Then I think we should take one with us.
A Shall I do that or will you?
B Leave that to me.
A I'm going to bring some samples, so I'll need a display stand.
B That's no problem. I'll bring one of those too.
A Do you think I should show them the new schedule?
B Yes, I do. And they're going to ask a lot of questions about delivery times, so be prepared.
A How do you know?
B They say so in their briefing notes. Haven't you read them?
A I've been very busy.
B But Bob, the notes tell you what they're going to ask.
A OK, I'll look through them tonight. Are you staying to watch my presentation?
B It'll be difficult. I've got to meet someone for lunch.
A I think there should be two of us there.
B I'll explain. They'll understand.
A I'm not very happy about it. You shouldn't leave a presentation half-way through.

PRONUNCIATION

3 A Who's got the list?
    B I can't fill it.
    C I don't want to sleep.
    D Where does he live?
    E Who's got the least?
    F I can't feel it.
    G I don't want to slip.
    H Where does he leave?

5   Growth and Development

PRESENTATION

A How long has SOFTBANK been in business?

B The company started in 1981. At that time the PC was just a toy. No one was distributing software. No one even knew what software was available.

A The growth's been phenomenal, then.

B That's right. Sales revenues have gone up every year since we started. At one time they were doubling every month.

A What's the main growth area now?

B Networking. That's really taking off. It includes operating systems, cables, boards, everything you need for the networked company. Before that, the big growth area was business applications. Things like word processing packages and spreadsheets.

A And before that?

B Games. Games software. That's where it all started.

A And what about your magazine business. Is that growing?

B Yes indeed. We published 14 different computer magazines last month. But it got off to a poor start initially.

A Yeah?

B We set up the publishing division just six months after we'd set up the distribution business, so we didn't have a lot of money to spare. We launched two magazines, printed 50,000 copies and 85% were returned.

A Really?

B They just didn't sell and they were eating up all our profits.

A I'm surprised you didn't close them down.

B We didn't want people to think we were in trouble. We decided to take a gamble instead. We made them twice as thick, kept the price the same, changed the layout and printed twice as many. Then we spent all the money we had left on TV advertising.

A It obviously worked.

B Yes. They sold out in three days.

LISTENING

1 Originally there were just two types of LEGO brick: one with four studs and one with eight. And they weren't very successful. The retailers weren't sure whether they would be able to sell them so we had to offer them on sale or return. And they sent quite a few boxes back to the factory.

2 We've been in business for over 60 years. The company was founded in Billund in Denmark by Ole Kirk Christiansen. He was the village carpenter and he started out selling wooden stepladders. He always had a lot of little bits of wood left over, so he started making them into wooden toys.

3 When Ole Kirk died he was succeeded by his son, Godtfred Kirk. Godtfred started working in the company when he was twelve years old and his father was just setting up the business. So he was the natural person to take over. We've always been a family company.

4 This was a real turning point for the company. The idea started when Godtfred Kirk met a toy buyer for one of the large department stores. They were talking about the toy market and the buyer told him about a theory he had. He felt that what the toy market lacked was a toy with a system. It had to be based on a sound idea, it had to be high quality and it had to develop children's imaginations. Godtfred realized our plastic building bricks had this potential and decided to develop the range. So we created the LEGO system of play and launched it in the buyer's store.

5 It was a disaster. It was insured for DKr 52,000 — a lot of money in those days — but it wasn't enough to cover the cost of reconstruction and re-equipping. It meant starting from scratch again. And there were 15 employees by then who all depended on the company. It was probably the saddest moment of Ole Kirk's career.

6 This is still our biggest market today. The original sales company was set up by a toy manufacturer, Axel Thomsen. Axel was so attracted to the idea of the LEGO play system that he sold his own factory so that he could spend all his time introducing LEGO products to the German market.

7 Ole Kirk offered a bottle of home-made wine as a prize to the person who suggested the best name. In fact he won it himself by combining the Danish words LEG GODT, meaning 'play well'. Later on he discovered that in Latin Lego means 'I put together' or 'I assemble'. Quite a coincidence, eh?

8 We were the first toy company in Denmark to use plastic. In fact we had a visit from the Danish toy trade magazine at the time and they wrote an article about it saying 'Plastics will never take the place of good, solid wooden toys'. Fortunately we didn't listen to their advice!

PRONUNCIATION

founded /ɪd/
adopted /ɪd/
destroyed /d/
purchased /t/
manufactured /d/
launched /t/
established /t/
died /d/
succeeded /ɪd/

6   Problem Solving

PRESENTATION

Conversation 1

A How about taking the Metro?

B I'm not sure about that. These are heavy.

A Do you have any French currency on you?

B Only about a hundred francs.

A Why don't we take a taxi and ask the driver to stop at a bank on the way?

B That's a good idea. What's the fare into the centre?

A More than a hundred francs, I'm sure. And they'll expect a tip.

163

B OK. We'll ask the driver to stop.

Conversation 2

A We've undercharged them.

B Really?

A Yes, have a look at the invoice. It doesn't include the legal fees or our agent's commission.

B Oh no! Have they paid this yet?

A Yes, last week.

B We'd better phone them up and explain what's happened.

Conversation 3

A It's the motor.

B So we can't fix it?

A We could try. But if we take the back off, it'll break the terms of the guarantee.

B Then I don't think we should. I'll call a service engineer.

A That might be the answer. How much do they charge for a call out?

B I'll find out.

Conversation 4

A Look, you can see. We're four days behind schedule. I think we should put everyone on overtime.

B If we did that, the wages and salary bill would shoot up.

A Just for a few weeks.

B No, it's simply not feasible. You'll have to rearrange this schedule to make up the lost time.

Conversation 5

A They're exactly what we need. The only problem is the price.

B How much do they cost?

A $60.

B If we buy 30, what discount will they give us?

A 10%.

B What if we bought 100?

A We'd get a higher discount, but we'd never be able to sell them all.

PRONUNCIATION

1 A That head-hunter phoned for you again today.

B Don't worry. If he offers me a job, I'll refuse.

2 A Another building firm's gone bankrupt.

B If the recession continues, we'll all be out of business.

3 A They're thinking of relocating their headquarters.

B If they moved up north, it'd be easier to attract staff.

4 A Don't miss your flight, whatever you do.

B I know. If I arrive late, they'll be furious.

5 A We need to keep our prices as low as possible.

B If energy costs increased, we'd have to raise them.

6 A They're planning to make more job cuts.

B If they made me redundant, I'd start my own business.

LISTENING

I had a terrible stock control problem with one of the shop managers. I used to say, 'Look, I don't want your stock in the stockroom — I want it on the shelves', but he never listened. He had a huge stockroom and every shelf was full.

Anyway, one day I'd had enough so I got hold of a carpenter and I boarded up his stockroom. You should have heard the screams, but that shop ran like clockwork after that.

1 The mixing machines ran 24 hours a day and we only turned them off at weekends. The lids had to be cleaned every day, so there were big safety guards to protect the operators' hands. It was hard work and the operators kept removing the guards to make it easier. I kept saying 'This is dangerous. You're crazy', but they wouldn't listen. Whenever I saw someone removing a safety guard, I'd wait and watch. Then, when their hand was stretched out over the lid, I'd throw the Off switch. They were big machines and they made an enormous noise when they stopped. It frightened the life out of the operators, I can tell you. They never took the guards off again after that.

2 The pay negotiations were going badly. We wanted to link the pay increase to a productivity deal, but the unions refused. They wouldn't budge. We finally reached a point where they were threatening to go on strike.

We sacked all the employees. We sent out letters to everyone saying that their employment would cease on a certain date. Then we offered them new employment contracts which linked a pay rise with productivity. One by one they all gave in and signed on the dotted line.

3 A professional organization in Hong Kong asked me to speak at one of their conferences. I'd never been to Hong Kong before so I was pretty excited. But I wasn't sure how much to charge — my normal fee plus air fare, or more, or less. I hadn't got a clue.

I asked them how many people they expected to come along and how much per head they would be paying. I discovered it was an enormous affair. I charged three times my normal fee and they never questioned it.

7 Telephoning to Exchange Information

PRESENTATION

A I've got a few queries about the invoice that you sent.

B Right. Fire away.

A Before we start, did you say it covers two shipments?

B Yes, that's right.

A Well, I've only received one so far. Could you tell me when you dispatched the second one?

B On the twenty-first.

A And do you know whether it includes the Rapidex plugs?

B Yes, 800, reference number G978.

A Ah, there's a problem there.

B Yes?

A I'm afraid we ordered the wrong size. We need the 7.92mm. That's J978.

B Not to worry. We'll dispatch them today. Just send the others back.

A Thanks. Now the next thing is the Posilock connectors.

B They were in the first shipment, which was dispatched on the 17th.

A Yes, they've arrived, but we ordered 3,500, not 3,000.

B Oh dear. I don't know how that happened. We'll send the rest immediately. Was there anything else?

A Yes. I also wanted a word about our discount. The person I spoke to when I placed the order said we might be able to have 10%, not 8%.

B I'm afraid I'm not authorized to change it. Mrs Cusimano's the person who deals with that, and I'm afraid she's not here at the moment.

A Have you any idea when she'll be back?

B I'm not sure, but I'll get her to phone you as soon as she comes in.

A OK. My name is Montano by the way, not Mondano. That's M-O-N-T-A-N-O.

B Right, Mr Montano. Sorry about that.

A OK, so could we run over that again to check? You're going to dispatch 800 Rapidex plugs reference number J978, not the G978, which we're going to send back when they arrive.

PRONUNCIATION

1

A I've got that address you wanted.

B Oh good.

A Ready?

B Yes.

A It's Avenida do Zimbabwe. That's A-V-E-N-I-D-A, new word ...

B Hang on. Was that A-V-E-N-E-D-A?

A No, A-V-E-N-I-D-A. Then D-O, new word, Z-I-M-B-A-B-W-E. Got that?

3

1 Can I check I've got it right. Her name's Culesza. That's C-U-L-E-S-Z-A?

2 Can I read that back to you? The town's called Maijar. That's M-A-I J-A-R.

3 Could we run over that again? His name is Rangit. That's R-A-N-G-I-T.

4 So it's called Harrai, H-A-R-R-A-I.

5 Did you say A-B-E-L-O-N?

8 Visitors

PRESENTATION

Conversation 1

A Hi. I have an appointment with Peter De Vuyst.

B Could I have your name?

A Sure. Here's my card.

B Right, Mrs Sandbulte. Would you like to take a seat?

A I'm in a hurry, actually. May I go straight up? I know the way.

B I'm afraid you'll need security clearance first.

A I see.

B It will take a few minutes, I'm afraid. There's fresh coffee over there if you'd like a cup while you wait.

A Yes, please. Don't worry. I'll help myself.

B OK, I'll call Mr De Vuyst.

Conversation 2

A Ulla! Kjell! It's lovely to see you both. Do come in.

B Thanks.

C Here. Let me take your coats.

D Thank you.

B I'm terribly sorry we're late. It was difficult to find a parking space.

A That's all right.

C Parking's always difficult around here.

D These are for you, Louise.

A Chrysanthemums! They're lovely.

D I'm glad you like them.

A I'll pop them in water straight away.

C Do come through to the living-room. Follow me. Now what would you like to drink?

D Well, I'm driving so I'd better have a mineral water or something like that.

Conversation 3

A Thanks for helping me find the platform.

B You're welcome. Do you want a hand with the other case?

A No, I can manage, thanks. There. Well, we must say goodbye. Thank you very much for having me.

B It's been a pleasure. Thank you for coming.

A Not at all.

B I think there's a restaurant car at the front of the train.

A Thanks, but I don't feel like eating just yet.

B Oh, I nearly forgot.

A What's this?

B That book you wanted. Do you remember?

A How kind. Now I insist on paying for this.

B Nonsense.

A No, please. How much did it cost?

Conversation 4

A Good shot! Well done.

B That was lucky. I'm not usually very good at hitting those long shots.

A Really?

B So, how much longer are you staying, Sam?

A Just four more days.

B Oh, that's a pity. Still, I expect you're looking forward to getting back to Michigan.

A Yeah.

B Have you been to Lyon yet?

A No, I'm going tomorrow.

B Good. You mustn't leave without visiting our plant there. Have you been before?

A No, never. I'm interested in seeing what you're doing there.

B Mmm. You'll like it. I think you need a three iron for this one.

A Would you pass it to me?

B Of course ... It's impossible to see the green from here, isn't it? Oh, hard luck!

Conversation 5

A Good afternoon. Can I help you?

B Yes. I'm thinking of extending my stay by a couple of days. Would you check if it's OK?

A Certainly.

B I'm Mrs Haberland, room 312.

A One moment.

B Instead of leaving on the fourteenth, I'd leave on the sixteenth.

A That's no problem. Shall I change the booking for you?

B No, it isn't definite yet. Could I confirm tonight?

A Yes, of course.

B And are there any messages for me?

A No, I'm afraid not.

B Are you quite certain?

A Ah, sorry. There's a fax.

B Thank you.

A Sorry about that.

B It's all right.

LISTENING

A Are we having a starter as well or just a main course?

B It's up to you. I think I can manage a starter though.

A I might have the avocado then. Prawns are a type of shellfish, aren't they?

B That's right.

A What about pancakes?

B They're like crêpes. And spinach is a dark green leafy vegetable. Have you ever tried stilton?

A I don't think so. What is it?

B It's a traditional English blue

cheese.

A Sounds nice. I think I'll have that instead. What are you having?

B I'll find out what the soup of the day is, then I'll have that or the melon. I like sorbet ... If you want something else that's very English, you could try the Beef Wellington.

A Where's that?

B Down in the main courses.

A Ah yes. Scottish beef. Could you explain the word 'turbot'.

B Turbot. Yes, it's a kind of flat fish. And it's covered with oatmeal, that's a flour made from oats.

A Oats?

B They use them to make porridge in Scotland. Have you ever had porridge?

A No, it doesn't matter. I think I'd like the lamb, anyway.

B Well I'm going to have the chicken.

A Stir-fried with beanshoots and ginger. It sounds Chinese.

B Yes, I like Chinese food. Do you?

A Yes. Have you ever tried Japanese food?

9 Reporting on Progress

PRESENTATION

A We planned to have this equipment in operation by week twelve. What's gone wrong?

B It's not our fault.

C We dislike changing the schedule as much as you.

B The suppliers have let us down. They guaranteed to deliver and install the equipment within five weeks of receiving our order.

A When did you place the order?

C At the end of week five. But now they say it will take six weeks.

A What's happened?

C As you know, we chose to prepare the site ourselves. The suppliers say we haven't done a good enough job.

A Is it true?

B No. We think some of their parts were faulty.

A Did they deliver on schedule?

C Yes, everything arrived at the end of week eight, but it's taken them a long time to get started.

B Of course they deny having problems with their parts. They've been blaming the site.

A Have they managed to get started now?

B Yes, but they won't finish installing it until the end of week eleven.

A But that's another two weeks.

B I know.

A So how does this affect the training schedule?

C We've recruited all the operators now and they've had one week of training so far. We can carry on giving them theoretical training, but they also need hands on experience.

B And we can't give them that until the equipment's installed.

C And we can't risk changing over to the new equipment without a full week of tests.

A So this date for the change-over — you want to put it off for a week?

C I'm afraid we can't avoid it.

LISTENING

A The time is six o'clock and here is Business Update with Gavin Scott.

B Unemployment has risen to over three million for the first time in six years and analysts expect the jobless total to rise by a further 40,000 this month. Manufacturing output has meanwhile steadied, after a nought point five per cent decrease last month. It is thought that today's rise in the unemployment figures could put pressure on the Prime Minister to cut interest rates, though the Bank of England have denied that this is likely.

B Guinness, Britain's largest drinks group, has announced plans to make 700 staff redundant at its United Distillers subsidiary in Scotland. Union officials have said the job losses are unnecessary. Claire Travers reports.

C The redundancies are part of a move by Guinness to improve productivity. But the news of the redundancies has been badly received here in Scotland. I spoke to some of the workers at a United Distillers factory.

D 'It's unnecessary, isn't it? Guinness are always saying we're the world's most profitable spirits company.'

E 'Aye. We're making a profit. We're not making a loss.'

F 'It's devastating. It will destroy entire communities.'

C Guinness strongly deny that communities will collapse as a result of the job losses. They say

they will improve investment and business. The group's cost-cutting measures also extend to Spain, where they will make job cuts at Cruzcampo, Spain's largest brewer, employing 30,000 people. Guinness bought Cruzcampo two years ago to expand into the fast-growing Spanish economy. The Spanish beer market shrank by about five per cent last year.

B The tobacco industry has today hit back at the Department of Health about cigarette advertising. They've issued a report arguing that cigarette advertisements do not encourage people to smoke more, and that they only encourage people to switch brands. The report is based on data collected from more than 90 countries around the world. It conflicts with figures issued by the Department of Health last month, which suggested that banning advertisements would result in a drop in consumption. A spokesperson for the tobacco industry said 'If a product is legally available, then it should be legal to advertise it.'

B The Conservative MP, David Willett, has called for the government to raise the state retirement age to 67 for both men and women. In a report published today by the Social Market Foundation, Mr Willett argues that raising the pension age would cut at least £5 billion from the Social Security budget. He also suggests that some of the savings should be ploughed back into higher state pensions for the over-eighties.

B And finally, in preparation for the introduction of high-speed trains, British Rail is recruiting volunteers for an unusual job. Ruth Mallon has the details.

H British Rail's volunteers will be tied to posts next to railway lines while high-speed trains pass by at 140 m.p.h. The experiment is designed to test the effects of turbulence, and British Rail hope to establish whether it is feasible for maintenance teams to work while the new trains are running. Many British Rail staff have already volunteered for the tests, and surprisingly, so have more than 50 members of the public. A British Rail spokesperson said 'People have been ringing in to say "We think it sounds exciting and we'd like to try it" ". One caller described it as the railway equivalent to bungee-jumping. British Rail has thanked all volunteers, but say they will only be using experienced staff.

B And that's all for today. The next news is at seven o'clock and we'll be back again at six o'clock tomorrow with Business Update.

PRONUNCIATION

1 news   move   *book*   two
2 cut   *suit*   some   truck
3 won   but   *met*   touch
4 *shoot*   good   put   should
5 must   *look*   once   luck
6 spend   *come*   meant   left

10 Describing Trends

PRESENTATION

1 As you can see, sales have risen gradually over the last five years. This growth is largely due to the record levels of sunshine we have enjoyed in recent years. This may be a result of global warming and so it could continue, but climatic trends are difficult to predict. For this reason we have made a fairly conservative projection for next year.

2 Toiletry sales through supermarkets are rising rapidly, but this has not been the trend with our sun-care products. In fact, sales through supermarkets have fallen slightly. Sales through department stores have remained steady and there's been a sharp increase in sales through chemists. We expect this trend to continue because consumers are becoming increasingly aware of the health issues involved in sunbathing. The number of people contracting skin cancer has doubled for the last two decades and there's a growing demand for sun-care products that offer greater protection.

3 As you can see, we've been able to reduce this budget and still improve our turnover. Our experiment with TV shots four years ago did not lead to significantly higher sales. Since then we have been steadily raising the proportion of spending

devoted to press advertising. This enables us to target consumers with high incomes, who will be more likely to take holidays abroad.

4 Demographic changes will probably have an adverse effect on the market in the future. The population is ageing and it's likely that this will have a negative influence. The 21-to-30 age group are traditionally heavy users of sun creams and this group is declining in numbers. Also usage is very low among the 50 plus age groups and these groups are expanding.

5 Sun protection creams and lotions account for the largest part of our turnover, but after-sun preparations are becoming slightly more important, as this pie chart shows. The new green and cruelty-free brand that we launched last year is selling well and this sector will definitely grow over the next few years to become a significant niche market.

PRONUNCIATION

1 There was a small decrease in sales.
2 We import some of our parts from China.
3 These cases are for export.
4 Have you made much progress?
5 We record all these transactions separately.
6 I'd like a refund please.

11 Products and Services

PRESENTATION

A The new motor's got to be reliable. And it's got to be efficient — low running costs are essential. Do you think you can do it?
B Yes. The key thing is to keep the temperature low.
A That's right. Your main problem will be the cooling system. It must be cooled by water.
B On the other hand, the working environment is very clean. We don't have to worry about dust and dirt.
A You have to solve the vibration problem, too.
B Yes, it mustn't vibrate above the limits, but that needn't be a major problem.

A Good. So what's the next step?
B Well, we've identified the design objectives now. Once you've written the specifications, I'll do some sketches.
A Should we meet again at that stage?
B Yes, we ought to. Then I can show you the different options.
A Will you have price estimates by then?
B Yes, I'll be able to give you a pretty accurate breakdown of costs. We'll discuss all the different options. Then you need to select the best ones.
A OK.
B After that, I'll draw up detailed designs.
A How quickly can you get the sketches ready? Can you do them in a week?
B I'm afraid I can't.
A Can't you get someone to help you?
B Yes I can, but it won't save much time. I'll need at least two weeks, I'm afraid.

12 Comparing Options

PRESENTATION

A James Jarvie.
B James, this is Catherine. I'm phoning about the autumn catalogue.
A Have you done the costings?
B Yes. I've got two estimates — one for printing in Hong Kong and one for printing in Europe.
A Yes?
B I've calculated on the basis of 368 pages, the same as last year.
A Yes, that's right. How do they compare?
B Europe's much more expensive. The printing costs are far lower in Hong Kong.
A Yes, they say Europe has the highest prices. But what about freight?
B Well, that's more from Hong Kong, of course. It's only a thousand pounds from Europe but it's three and a half thousand from Hong Kong. On the other hand, that's only a small part of the bill.
A And delivery? If we order next week, when will they get here?
B Europe's quicker obviously. Just two weeks. It takes six from Hong Kong.

167

A But even if it takes six weeks, we'll still be in time for the September mailing.

B Exactly. Of course, there's another factor.

A What's that?

B The exchange rate. I've used a rate of one pound to eleven Hong Kong dollars.

A Then we ought to buy dollars now, in case the rate changes.

B I can't do that until I've got the go-ahead from head office.

A I'm going there this afternoon. You could give me the figures and I'll have a word with Finance when I see them.

B OK. In Hong Kong, the total production costs work out at two pounds fifty-one a copy. Got that?

A Uh huh.

B And they're two pounds seventy a copy in Europe.

A Europe's *much* dearer, isn't it?

B Yes, unless the Hong Kong dollar rises dramatically in the next few days.

A Don't worry. I'll tell them we need a quick decision.

B Thanks, James.

LISTENING

Building team spirit is always the focal point of what I try to do as a manager. When I first went to Crystal Palace, players would finish training and then go straight home. There was no atmosphere. So we brought in a pool table and fruit machines. When players choose to spend time together, it generates a better atmosphere.

The team spirit's very important, but I don't believe in trying to motivate the team as a team. I try to motivate them as individuals. So I don't give team talks. I speak to the players individually. And I try not to put too much pressure on them. I believe players perform best when they are relaxed. If they're too tense, I can guarantee they won't play well.

I also believe in giving people autonomy. I like all the people who work for me to be autonomous. I very rarely interfere. I feel people should be judged on their results. If they prove incompetent, then I'm incompetent if I keep on employing them.

It's like that with the team. I get criticized for not interfering during a game and making more substitutions.

But I feel if I've chosen those eleven players to get a result, then I should leave them alone to get on with it.

If I'm dropping a player from the team, I don't feel I have to explain it to them. If they want to discuss it, I'll say 'Come back and talk about it in a couple of days time.' But I don't try to re-motivate them. It's up to them to have the character to fight back. I'm a great believer that almost everything you achieve in life is down to your attitude. If I have a player who is magnificently gifted but has a stinking attitude, I won't waste my time on them.

13 Meetings

PRESENTATION

Part 1

A I understand there's a problem with the prototype. Could you fill us in, Sarah?

B Yes, of course. It all began when the designer had to incorporate a smaller battery. When he was altering the design, he moved a socket.

C Didn't he check with Production first?

B I'm afraid not. If he had, we wouldn't have had all these problems.

A Could you tell us more about the problems?

B Yes. We're having trouble locating the holes. There's a limit to how precise we can be with the tooling equipment.

A So are you saying we can't produce the new design?

B I'm afraid so.

C Didn't anyone notice the mistake?

B Yes, the engineers realized they couldn't meet the new specifications.

A So what did they do?

B They changed the tolerances to fit their tools.

A Do you mean they altered the design?

B That's right. Then they built the prototype.

C So if they'd checked first, we'd have avoided all these problems.

B Yes, but unfortunately they didn't.

Part 2

B So the prototype doesn't work. It's a real headache.

A I think we should go back to the drawing-board. Do you have any views on this, Lance?

C I'm not sure. What do you think, Sarah?

B If we went back to stage one, we'd lose a lot of time. It'd take weeks to get this far again.

C If you worked on the prototype, could you get it to function?

B Yes, but it wouldn't meet all the specifications.

C But it'd meet most of them?

A What do you mean, Lance? Are you suggesting we play about with the existing designs instead of starting again?

C I'm not sure. It'd mean we'd save time.

B But we'd have to accept a lower-quality product.

PRONUNCIATION

1 meet mean *it* be
2 change say *said* rate
3 work firm heard *draw*
4 fill *feel* will built
5 *they* check debt lend
6 sure four *word* more

14 Presentations

PRESENTATION

Part 1

Paul I'm very pleased to welcome Eva Lundqvist from Market Intelligence. As you know, she has been doing a lot of research into where we should be advertising. So Eva, would you like to fill us in?

Eva Of course. Thank you, Paul. Er ... how much time have we got?

Paul Only a little, I'm afraid.

Eva Well in that case, I'll begin straight away with a few of our survey results. Can everyone see this all right?

Paul Yes.

Roger Yes, it's fine.

Eva OK. As you can see, the question we asked was 'Which of these types of newspaper have you read in the last six months?' The most popular choice was a daily newspaper. 65% had read a national tabloid in the last six months. And then moving on to Sunday newspapers. 51% of the sample had read a tabloid, so that was about half.

Roger Er, sorry. How big was the sample? How many people did you question?

Eva Just under a thousand.

Roger OK. And 4% had read no paper.

Eva That's right. Can I draw your attention to the weekly papers, though? 8% of the sample had read a regional paid-for paper.

Paul Not very many.

Eva No, but I'd like to come back to that later ... OK, let's turn to the results we got for ...

Part 2

Eva It doesn't cost much to advertise in the regional papers, though the national papers have larger circulations.

Roger So Eva, can I get this clear? Do you recommend we advertise in the national tabloids?

Eva No. I advise you to advertise in the papers that attract the right sort of readers. We need to look more closely at the consumers. Let me move on to this profile ...

OK. This shows the percentage of adults who have read a regional paid-for paper in the last six months.

Paul It's only 8%.

Eva That's true. But as you can see, these papers attract older readers. 13% are aged between forty-five and fifty-four. Remember, old consumers have more money to spend than the younger ones. And look at this. 12% of the readers are in the AB socio-economic group. I suggest you concentrate your efforts on these weekly papers. There isn't much point in advertising in papers that attract the wrong groups.

PRONUNCIATION

4

Good afternoon everyone./As you know/I'm here to tell you about/British Telecom's/video conferencing facilities./ I'd like to start by explaining/how video conferences work./Then I'll turn/ to our facilities in the UK/–first/our existing locations/then/the planned new ones.

Grammar and Usage Notes

THE PRESENT SIMPLE TENSE

FORM

- Add an *s* to the third person singular form.

I You We They	work	
		at weekends.
He She It	works	

- Use *do* as a help verb to make negative sentences and questions.

I You We They	do not work don't work	
		at weekends.
He She It	does not work doesn't work	

Do	I you we they	
		work at weekends?
Does	he she it	

- Use *do* as a help verb in short answers.

Do you work at weekends?
*No, I **don't**.*
Does she work on Saturdays?
*Yes, she **does**.*

USES

1 To talk about regular activities

a **Habits and Routines (1)**
Branson starts work around eight and doesn't finish until seven at night.

b **Timetables and schedules (7)**
The train for Geneva leaves at 7.30.
The banks don't open on Saturdays.

2 To describe things that stay the same

a **Long-term activities (1) (3)**
I live in France but I work in Switzerland.
The company owns a contemporary art gallery.

b **Opinions and feelings (13)**
What do you think of the plan?
I like Chinese food.

c **Things that are always true (facts) (3)**
It rains a lot in Seattle.
We come from Eberswalde.

NOTES

☞ See the notes on the Present Continuous tense (page 172) for comparison.

The numbers in brackets refer to units of the book that contain more examples.

THE PRESENT CONTINUOUS TENSE

FORM

- Use the verb *be* and *-ing*. Don't forget to use contractions when speaking.

I	am 'm	
You We They	are 're	working.
He She It	is 's	

- Use *not* to make negative sentences.

I	'm not	
You We They	aren't 're not	working.
He She It	isn't 's not	

- Use the verb *be* in short answers.
  Are you working on this project?
  Yes, I am.
  And is he?
  No, he isn't.

USES

1 To talk about things that are happening now

a **Things that are happening at the time of speaking (2)**
Who's calling please?
I am writing to confirm our order no. 65732.

b **Temporary activities happening around the time of speaking (3) (10)**
AT&T is streamlining its operations and reducing costs at the moment.
Many governments are reducing expenditure on defence.

2 To talk about future plans and arrangements (2)
She's arriving at 11 o'clock.
I'm coming to England next week.

NOTES

Compare the present simple and continuous tenses in these examples.

I work in New York. (I'm based there permanently.)
I'm working in London for a few weeks. (I'm based there temporarily.)

I play golf every Saturday. (habitual activity)
I'm playing golf this Saturday. (future plan)

I think the President will resign. (opinion)
I'm thinking about the problem. (activity happening now)

The numbers in brackets refer to units of the book that contain more examples.

THE PRESENT PERFECT TENSE

FORM

I Simple

• Use *have* as a help verb with the third part of the verb (the past participle). Make negative sentences with *not*.

I You We They	have haven't	
He She It	has hasn't	**begun** the job.

2 Continuous

• Use *have* as a help verb with *been* and *-ing*. Use *not* to make negative sentences.

I You We They	have haven't	
He She It	has hasn't	**been working** all night.

• Change the word order to form questions.

Has it taken long?
How long have you been working here?

• Use the help verb *have* in short answers.

Has she been waiting long? – *Yes, she **has**.*
Have you known him long? – *No, I **haven't**.*

For information on the different uses of the simple and continuous forms of the Present Perfect, see page 92.

USES

I To talk about actions that started in the past and are still continuing (5)

He's been living in Tokyo since 1991.
I've been working in Paris for the last two months.
How long have you had this job?

In this use the simple and continuous forms have virtually the same meaning.

2 To talk about finished past actions (8) (9)

We use the present perfect to talk about finished past actions that are still important at the time of speaking. We are not interested in when the actions happened. We're just interested in their effects on the present. The time reference is indefinite.

a Life experiences (8)
I've seen her several times before so I know what she looks like.
Have you seen Herr Wick? I can't find him.
I've never eaten sushi. What's it like?
In this use we usually use the simple form.

b Past actions with present results (9)
I've written the report. You can have it now.
He's been overworking. That's why he's tired.
We often use the Present Perfect to give news of recent events.
Guinness has announced plans to make 700 staff redundant.
I've just heard. We've won the export award.

NOTES

Compare the use of the Present Perfect and Simple Past tense in these sentences.
I've been living in France for six years. (I still live there.)
I lived in Hong Kong for two years. (I don't live there any more.)

Have you ever been to Russia? (Indefinite time)
Yes, I went to Moscow six years ago. (Definite time)

The numbers in brackets refer to units of the book that contain more examples.

THE PAST SIMPLE TENSE

FORM

* Regular verbs end in -*ed*.
She worked here for six years.
We launched two magazines and printed 50,000 copies.
For information on the pronunciation of the -*ed* endings see page 55.

* Many common English verbs have irregular past tense forms.
It was difficult.
We took a gamble.
They sold out in three days.
See page 188 for a list of irregular verbs.

* Use *did* to make negatives, questions, and short answers.
They didn't start on time.
Did they deliver on schedule? – Yes, they did.

USE

To talk about finished past actions (5) (9) (13)
We sent the shipment on the 14th.
It arrived two days late.

NOTES

☞ See the comparison with the Past Continuous on page 174, the Past Perfect on page 175 and the Present Perfect on page 173.

THE PAST CONTINUOUS TENSE

FORM

* Use the past tense of the verb *be* and -*ing*.
I was talking to her for an hour.

* Change the word order to form a question.
What were you talking about?

* Use *not* to make negative sentences.
I wasn't talking for long.

* Use *was* and *were* in short answers.
Was he staying at the Hilton? – Yes, he was.
Were you staying long?   – No, we weren't.

USES

1 **To describe previous plans (2)**
   We were going on a workshop tour at two but I've cancelled it.

2 **To describe the background circumstances of a past event (5)**
   I went to Saudi in '92. At that time, we were looking for an agent to sell our products in the Middle East.

3 **To describe incomplete or interrupted past actions (5)**
   I was leaving the office when the telephone rang. I stopped to answer it.

The numbers in brackets refer to units of the book that contain more examples.

NOTES

We use the past simple to talk about completed past actions.

He met his wife in 1975.

But we use the past continuous to talk about actions that were in progress at a particular time in the past.

He met his wife while he was living in America.

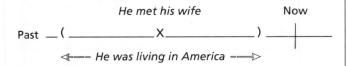

We also use the past continuous to talk about incomplete actions. Compare the simple and continuous forms in these sentences.

The company went out of business when she became the Managing Director. She made some bad decisions which led to bankruptcy.
(One action followed the other.)

The company was going out of business when she became the Managing Director. She made some good decisions and turned it round.
(One action interrupted the other.)

THE PAST PERFECT TENSE

FORM

The form is the same as the Present Perfect tense but with *had* as a help verb, instead of *have*. (The help verb *had* is often shortened to *'d*.)

USES

1   To show that one action in the past happened before another (5)

We set up the publishing division just six months after we had set up the distribution business.

2   To report what people said or thought in the past

He said he'd been in prison.
They'd always told us that our prices were high.

NOTES

Compare the Past Simple and Past Perfect in these examples.
We can use the Past Simple to talk about one event in the past.
He forgot to pick up his glasses.

We can use the Past Simple to talk about events that followed one another.
He left the office and drove to Scotland.

But we use the Past Perfect to talk about a second or earlier past time.
When he got to Scotland, he realized he had forgotten his glasses.

☞   See the notes on restricted conditionals on page 180.

The numbers in brackets refer to units of the book that contain more examples.

FUTURE TIME

We can use many different verb forms to talk about the future. Which one we choose depends on how we view a future action. We might see it as an intention or a future arrangement, or a prediction, and so on. Here are some important forms along with their uses:

USES	FORMS
1 Expressing intentions	
a Instant decisions made at the time of speaking. (4)	*will*
The line's engaged. – OK. I'll call back later.	
It's raining. – Then I'll call a taxi.	
b Decisions made before the time of speaking. (4)	*going to*
I've already decided. I'm going to resign.	
What are your plans? Are you going to stay and listen to my talk?	
2 Future plans and arrangements (2)	Present Continuous
I'm visiting the Harlow plant tomorrow.	
What time is she arriving?	
3 Timetables and schedules. (7)	Present Simple
The meeting starts at four o'clock.	
What time do the banks open?	
4 Predictions	
a Opinions and facts (3)	*will*
Business organizations will be leaner and flatter in the future.	
How many people will be at the meeting?	
b Predictions based on present evidence (4)	*going to*
I read the briefing notes. They're going to ask a lot of questions about delivery.	
Look at these figures. We're going to go bankrupt!	

NOTES

We can use both *will* and *going to* in future predictions. In this use, *will* is an ordinary help verb. It just signifies a future action and adds no extra meaning. *Going to* and *will* are interchangeable in many future predictions.

How many people will be at the meeting?
How many people are going to be at the meeting?

We often use *going to* when a prediction is based on evidence or we can see something is going to happen.

Look at those clouds. It's going to rain.
I've got lots of publicity material. I'm going to need a large display stand.

We also use a lot of modal verbs to talk about the future.

☛ See the notes on modal verbs on page 178.
We also use a lot of other expressions to talk about how probable or likely future events are.
☛ See the following section on Future Probability.

FUTURE PROBABILITY

Here are some common words and expressions for talking about how probable or likely events are in the future.

1 *probably* and *definitely* (10)

- The position of *probably* and *definitely* changes in positive and negative sentences.

The company	will probably will definitely probably won't definitely won't	make a loss this year.

2 *likely* (10)

- We can construct sentences with *likely* in several different ways.

The company	is likely to isn't likely to	make a loss.
It's likely that It isn't likely that	the company will	

3 *bound to* and *no chance* (10)

- Notice the gerund and infinitive forms in these two expressions.

*The company is bound **to make** a loss.*
(It's certain that it will.)
*There's no chance of the company **making** a loss.*
(It's certain that it won't.)

4 'Opinion verbs' (10)

- We use many different verbs to express opinions about how probable a future event is. Here are some examples:

I'm sure I don't doubt that I expect I think	the company will make a loss this year.
I doubt if I don't think	the company will make a profit this year.

5 *could*, *may*, and *might* (10)

- We use the modal verbs *could*, *may*, and *might* to talk about future possibilities.

The company	may might could	make a loss.

The numbers in brackets refer to units of the book that contain more examples.

MODAL VERBS

FORMS

• Use the modal verb with the stem of the main verb. Don't add -s in the third person singular.
*You **can** chair the meeting if she's away.*
*The bank **might** lend us the money.*

• Make a question by changing the word order.
***Could** you lend me some money?*
***May** I smoke?*

• Make a negative by adding *not* to the modal verb.

can't	*mustn't*
cannot	*shouldn't*
couldn't	*wouldn't*

But be careful; there are some exceptions.
1 *Will not* is very strong; *won't* is more common in spoken English.
2 *Mightn't*, *mayn't*, and *shan't* are very unusual.

• **Don't** use *do* as a help verb to make negatives and questions.
Can you speak Italian?
NOT   ~~Do you can speak Italian?~~
I can't drive.   NOT   ~~I don't can drive.~~

• **Don't** use *to* after modal verbs.
We must change the system.
NOT   ~~We must to change the system.~~

Modal	Examples	Uses
can	*They can control their own budgets.*	Ability / Possibility (11)
	We can't fix it.	Inability / Impossibility (11)
	Can I smoke here?	Asking for permission (7)
	Can you help me?	Request (8)
could	*Could I borrow your dictionary?*	Asking for permission (7)
	Could you say it again more slowly.	Request (8)
	We could try to fix it ourselves.	Suggestion (6)
	I think we could have another Gulf War.	Future possibility (10)
	He gave up his old job so he could work for us.	Ability in the past (5)
may	*May I have another cup of coffee?*	Asking for permission (7)
	China may become a major economic power.	Future possibility (10)
might	*They might give us a 10% discount.*	Future possibility (10)
will	*I can't see any taxis so I'll walk.*	Instant decisions (4)
	I'll do that for you if you like.	Offer (4)
	I'll get back to you first thing on Monday.	Promise (2)
	Profits will increase next year.	Prediction (3)
would	*Would you mind if I brought a colleague with me?*	Asking for permission (2)
	Would you pass the salt?	Request (2) (8)
	Would you mind waiting a moment?	Request (2) (8)
	'Would three o'clock suit you?' – 'That'd be fine.'	Making arrangements (2)
	Would you like to play golf this Friday?	Invitation (2) (8)
	'Would you prefer tea or coffee?' – 'I'd like tea, please.'	Preferences (2) (8)

Modal	Examples	Uses
shall	*Shall I help you with your baggage?*	Offer (8)
	Shall we say 2.30, then?	Suggestion (**8**)
	Shall I do that or will you?	Asking what to do (4)
should	*We should sort out this problem at once.*	Saying what's right or correct (4)
	I think we should check everything again.	Recommending action (4)
ought to	*We ought to employ a professional writer.*	Saying what's right or correct (4)
must	*We must say good-bye now.*	Necessity / Obligation (11)
	They mustn't disrupt the work more than necessary.	Prohibition (**11**)

The numbers in brackets refer to units of the book that contain more examples.

CONDITIONALS

FORMS

In many cases, the tenses used in conditional sentences are the same as those used in any other kind of sentence.

If you don't like it, you can leave.
If you're going upstairs, could you give this parcel to Julian?
If they've already signed the contract, it's too late to change anything.

But be careful. After *if*, we generally use a present tense to express a future idea. It is very unusual to use *will* in the same clause as *if*.
If I see her, I'll give her your message.
NOT   ~~If I will see her, I'll give her your message.~~

To talk about less likely situations, we use *if* with *would, could,* or *might.*

*If the EC **had** a common currency, it **might** solve a lot of problems.*
  past tense   *might* + stem

*If they **offered** me the job, I **couldn't** accept it.*
  past tense   *couldn't* + stem

Notice we use the past tense to express a present or future idea in the two sentences above.

We also use conditionals to talk about an imaginary situation in the past (something that **didn't** really happen). If we are talking about a hypothetical situation in the past, we use the past perfect tense.

*If you **had told** me about the meeting, I **would have** gone.*
  past perfect tense   *would* + present perfect tense

USES

If they offer me the job, I will accept it.
Possible condition (6)

If they offered me the job, I would accept it.
(...but I don't think they will offer it to me.)
Hypothetical condition (6) (13)

If they had offered me the job, I would have accepted it.
(...but they didn't offer it to me.)
Hypothetical condition in the past (13)

NOTES

1   **The *if*-clause can come at the beginning or the end of the sentence.**
    If they offer me the job, I'll accept.
    I'll accept if they offer me the job.

    A comma is more usual if the *if*-clause comes first.

2   **In possible conditions, we use *if* to talk about things that might happen.**
    If I see her, I'll give her your message.
    (I'm not sure I'll see her.)

    But if we are sure they will happen, we use *when.*
    When I see her, I'll give her your message.
    (I'm sure I'll see her.)

    If we are talking about conditions that are always true, *if* and *when* are interchangeable and we use the present tense in both clauses.

If	
When	*it's twelve o'clock in London, it's nine o'clock in Tokyo.*

If	
When	*the team is under pressure, it always performs badly.*

3   ***If* is not the only word we can use to express a condition.**
    *I won't ring you **unless** there are any problems.*
    Unless is similar to *if...not.* The sentence above means: *I'll ring you if there are any problems.*

    *I'll take the train **in case** the traffic's heavy.*
    In case is used with precautions that must be taken to prevent future problems. This sentence means: *The traffic might be heavy so I'll take the train.*
    See Unit 12 for more examples.

THE PASSIVE VOICE

FORM

● Use the verb *be* as a help verb. with the third part of the verb (the past participle.) Use the correct tense of the verb *be*.

Present Simple	The sauce **is made** of oranges.
Present Continuous	Seven hundred staff **are being made** redundant.
Past Simple	It **was invented** in 1938 by Chester Carlson.
Present Perfect	All the money in the safe **has been stolen.**
Past Continuous	The factory **was being built** when I last came here.
Future with *will*	A weak signal **will be emitted.**
Future with *going to*	A division **is going to be sold.**

● With verbs like *can, must, ought to*, etc., use the modal verb + *be* + the past participle.
*The company **should be taken** to court and punished.*
*That invoice **ought to be checked** carefully.*

USES

1 **To describe actions without saying who does them (11):**
The company was founded in 1928.
The eggs are made of chocolate.

2 **To describe processes (11)**
The data has to be collected, then it's analysed, and finally the results are published.

NOTES

You can use the passive voice and still say who or what performed an action by using *by*.
*Policy decisions are made **by** the Board of Directors.*
*The results are collated **by** the computer.*

But in many sentences this is unnecessary.
The password has been changed (by the network manager).

GERUNDS AND INFINITIVES

An infinitive is the 'to' form of a verb.
Examples: *to do, to work*
A gerund is a noun made from a verb by adding *-ing*.
Examples: *doing, working*

Compare these two sentences:
I like fast cars
   | |
 verb   noun

I like driving
   | |
 verb   gerund

1 **Gerunds follow prepositions in some common expressions (8)**
Examples: *I'm looking forward to **seeing** you.*
*I'm thinking of **visiting** the States next year.*

2 **Certain verbs can be followed by infinitives, but not gerunds (9)**
For your reference, here is a list of some common ones:
decide, want, plan, manage, choose, offer, promise, agree, can't afford, refuse, fail, learn

3 **Certain verbs can be followed by gerunds, but not infinitives (9)**
For your reference, here is a list of some common ones:
finish, enjoy, dislike, avoid, give up, deny, suggest, delay, put off, carry on, keep on, can't help, risk

4 **Certain verbs can be followed by gerunds or infinitives, but their meaning changes.**
Examples: *I stopped writing the report.*
(= I was writing the report, then I stopped.)
I stopped to write the report.
(= I stopped what I was doing in order to write the report.)

The numbers in brackets refer to units of the book that contain more examples.

NUMBERS

CARDINAL NUMBERS

These numbers are often confused. Notice that if we pronounce them singly, the stress changes.

16, 60	*six**teen**, **six**ty*
17, 70	*seven**teen**, **seven**ty*

In British English we say *and* before the tens in large numbers. This is left out in US English.

465	*four hundred (and) sixty-five*
701	*seven hundred (and) one*

A comma is often written to separate the thousands in numbers over 999.

3,986	*three thousand nine hundred and eighty-six.*

We sometimes say *a* instead of *one* in large numbers.

1,000,000	*a million*

British and US English differ in the pronunciation of these very large numbers.

1,000,000,000	*a thousand million* (British English)
	a billion (US English)
1,000,000,000,000	*a billion* (British English)
	a trillion (US English)

However, many British companies are now adopting the US usage, so if in doubt, check.

Some British newspapers have started to adopt the European term *milliard* to refer to a thousand million, but many British people are still unfamiliar with the term.

LONG NUMBERS

In long numbers such as phone, fax, bank account, or credit card numbers, we pronounce the figures individually.

720844	*seven two oh, eight double four*

We generally group the numbers in threes, rather than in twos as is common in Europe.

seven two oh/ eight double four

MONEY

Although the money signs are written in front of the numbers, we generally say them after the numbers.

FF56	*fifty-six French francs*
$4m	*four million dollars*
¥92bn	*ninety-two billion yen*

Do not make this common mistake:

~~Ninety-two billions of yen~~

We pronounce years in two halves.

1996	*nineteen ninety-six*

But we pronounce the year two thousand whole.

2001	*two thousand and one*

DATES

In British English *the* and *of* are spoken but not written.

25th April 1954
The twenty-fifth of April, nineteen fifty-four
or *April the twenty-fifth, nineteen fifty-four*

In US English the date is generally written with the month first and the date second. *The* and *of* are not usually used in the spoken form.

May 16 1996
May sixteenth, nineteen ninety-six

This can lead to misunderstandings when dates are given in figures only.

10.12.1995
The tenth of December nineteen-ninety-five (British English)
October twelfth, nineteen ninety-five (US English)

TIMES

A simple way to tell the time is to say the numbers.

7.30, 3.45, 1.20	*seven thirty, three forty-five, one twenty*

Alternatively, you can say:
Half past seven, a quarter to four, twenty past one

In US English, you can choose between two different prepositions.
Half past/after seven, quarter to/of four, twenty past/after one

We do not usually use the twenty-four hour clock unless we are talking about plane or train timetables.

14.00	*The meeting is at two o'clock.*
	The train leaves at fourteen hundred hours.

FRACTIONS

$\frac{1}{2}$, $\frac{3}{4}$, $1\frac{2}{3}$ *a half, three-quarters, one and two-thirds*

DECIMAL FRACTIONS

In British and US English, a point is used when writing decimals, not a comma as is common in Europe.

6.9   *six point nine*

0 is pronounced 'oh' after the point and 'nought' before the point in British English and 'zero' or 'oh' in US English.

8.07   *eight point oh seven* (British English)
     eight point zero seven (US English)
0.6   *nought point six* (British English)
     point six (US English)

The numbers after the point are pronounced individually.

24.35   *twenty-four point three five*

MEASUREMENTS

62km   *sixty-two kilometres*
14 $\frac{1}{2}$cm   *fourteen and a half centimetres*
6m x 9m   *six metres by nine metres*

Temperatures were traditionally measured in the Fahrenheit scale. Although the Celsius or centigrade scale is now officially in use, the Fahrenheit scale is still used informally for non-scientific purposes in Great Britain and the United States.

92°F   *ninety-two degrees Fahrenheit*
– 4°C   *minus four degrees Celsius/centigrade*

SUMS

15 + 6 = 21   *fifteen plus/and six equals twenty one*
32 – 24   *thirty two minus/take away/less twenty four*
6 x 8   *six multiplied by eight/times eight*
28 ÷ 7   *twenty-eight divided by seven*
5^2 *five squared*
$\sqrt{9}$ *the square root of nine*

SPORTS RESULTS

'Zero' in US English is usually pronounced *oh* or *nought* in British English. But in sports results, it can also be pronounced *nil* or *love*.
Football:
Real Madrid three; Ajax Amsterdam nil.
Tennis:
And it's Becker to serve with the score at fifteen love.

TIME PREPOSITIONS

Preposition	Time	Examples
in	parts of the day months seasons years	*(the) morning(s), (the) afternoon(s)* *June, February* *(the) winter, (the) autumn*[†] *1966, 1997*
at	times of the clock religious festivals points in time	*3.30 pm, half past two* *Christmas, Easter* *the weekend* *the beginning of March*
on	days dates	*[#]Thursday(s), Christmas Day* *2nd May, August 16th 1994*

[†]*autumn* = British English   *fall* = US English
[#]*I'll see you on Thursday.* (British)   *I'll see you Thursday.* (US)

POLITE EXPRESSIONS

FORMS AND USES

We use a lot of standard polite expressions in social situations. Here are examples of some important ones.

Asking people to do things (2) (4) (8)	Agreeing	Refusing
Can you... ?	Yes, certainly.	I'm sorry, but...
Will you... ?	Yes, of course.	I'm afraid...
Could you... ?	No, not at all.	
Would you... ?		
Could you possibly... ?		
Would you mind... (-ing) ?		

Asking for permission to do things (2) (8)	Agreeing	Refusing
Can I... ?	Yes, certainly.	I'm sorry, but...
Could I... ?	Yes, of course.	I'm afraid...
May I... ?	Please do.	
Could I possibly... ?	By all means.	
Would you mind if I... ?	No, not at all.	

Thanking (2) (8)	Replies
Thanks.	You're welcome.
Thank you very much indeed.	Don't mention it.
It's very good of you.	Not at all.
	It's a pleasure.

Apologizing (2) (8)	Replies
Sorry.	It's OK.
I'm extremely sorry.	No problem.
	It doesn't matter.
	Don't worry about it.

Offering help (1) (2) (4) (8)	Accepting	Refusing
Do you want a hand?	That'd be great.	No, it's all right thanks.
Can I... ?	Yes please. Thank you very much.	That's kind of you, but I can manage.
Shall I... ?		
Would you like me to... ?		

The numbers in brackets refer to the units of the book that contain more examples of practice activities.

Inviting people to do something themselves (8)	Accepting	Refusing
Please... Do...	Thank you.	I'm all right, thank you.

Inviting people to do something with you (2) (8)	Accepting	Refusing
Would you like to... ?	Thank you. I'd like that. That would be lovely.	I'd love to, but... I'm sorry, but...

NOTES

1 Request forms are listed with more informal examples at the top and more formal at the bottom. So, for example, we are more likely to use *Can you...?* if we are making a small request to someone we know well, and *Would you mind...?* when making a big request to someone we don't know well.

2 Notice we use different forms for asking people to do things and asking for permission to do things.

3 The word *mind* means object to or be annoyed by, so to agree to requests that contain this word you have to say *No*, or *No, not at all*.

4 The verb forms change in these two requests:
Would you mind lending me your pen?
(The verb is transformed into a gerund.)

Would you mind if I used your phone?
(We use a past tense form in this restricted conditional.)

5 If you're refusing a request, it's generally polite to give a reason.

6 We use the expression *Do you want a hand?* when we offer to work alongside someone.

7 We can invite someone to do something themselves by saying *please* or *do*.
Please sit down.
Do help yourself.

8 Simply saying 'yes' is not enough when you are accepting an invitation. It's important to sound positive and enthusiastic.

The numbers in brackets refer to the units of the book that contain more examples of practice activities.

LETTERS AND FAXES

Letters, the traditional form of business communication, are still generally preferred for confidential and very formal correspondence. But faxes (telefaxes) are growing in popularity, due to their speed and convenience. Many companies now have their own fax stationery which resembles a memo (memorandum) in layout. As information about the sender and receiver appears at the top, traditional greetings are often omitted so faxes tend to be more direct.

For information on layout, study the two documents below. For more examples, see pages 42-44. For standard phrases frequently used in letters and faxes, see page 44.

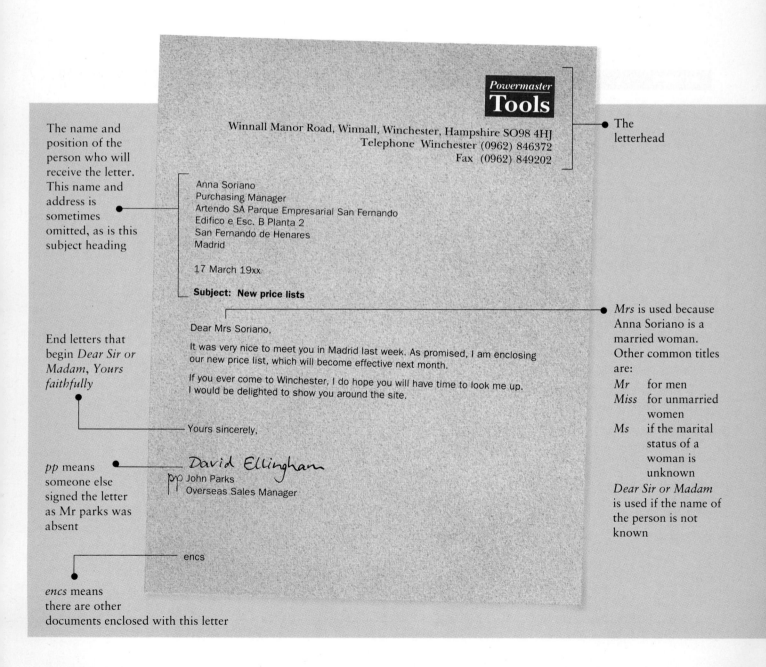

The name and position of the person who will receive the letter. This name and address is sometimes omitted, as is this subject heading

The letterhead

Powermaster Tools

Winnall Manor Road, Winnall, Winchester, Hampshire SO98 4HJ
Telephone Winchester (0962) 846372
Fax (0962) 849202

Anna Soriano
Purchasing Manager
Artendo SA Parque Empresarial San Fernando
Edifico e Esc. B Planta 2
San Fernando de Henares
Madrid

17 March 19xx

Subject: New price lists

Dear Mrs Soriano,

It was very nice to meet you in Madrid last week. As promised, I am enclosing our new price list, which will become effective next month.

If you ever come to Winchester, I do hope you will have time to look me up. I would be delighted to show you around the site.

Yours sincerely,

David Ellingham
pp John Parks
Overseas Sales Manager

encs

End letters that begin *Dear Sir or Madam*, *Yours faithfully*

pp means someone else signed the letter as Mr parks was absent

encs means there are other documents enclosed with this letter

Mrs is used because Anna Soriano is a married woman. Other common titles are:

Mr   for men
Miss   for unmarried women
Ms   if the marital status of a woman is unknown

Dear Sir or Madam is used if the name of the person is not known

TELEFAX TRANSMISSION

Winnall Manor Road, Winnall, Winchester, Hampshire SO98 4HJ
Telephone Winchester (0962) 846372
Fax (0962) 849202

To: Artendo SA   **Attention:**   Anna Soriano,
                                                   Purchasing Department

From: John Parks   **Subject:**   New price list

Date: 17/3/– –   **Pages (including this one):** six

Information about
the sender and
receiver

The number
of sheets to be
transmitted

Greetings are
often omitted
in faxes

It was very nice to meet you in Madrid last week. As promised, I am sending
our new price list, which will become effective next month.

If you ever come to Winchester, I do hope you will have time to look me up.
I would be most happy to show you around our site.

Best wishes,

John Parks

Yours sincerely and
Yours faithfully are
used less frequently
in faxes. *Best wishes,*
Kind regards, or
simply *Regards* are
common.

If you do not receive all the pages, please advise us as soon as possible.

In case of a
fault during
transmission

187

IRREGULAR VERBS

Stem	Past Tense	Past Participle
be	was /were	been
become	became	become
begin	began	begun
break	broke	broken
bring	brought	brought
build	built	built
buy	bought	bought
catch	caught	caught
choose	chose	chosen
come	came	come
cost	cost	cost
cut	cut	cut
deal	dealt	dealt
do	did	done
draw	drew	drawn
drink	drank	drunk
drive	drove	driven
eat	ate	eaten
fall	fell	fallen
feed	fed	fed
feel	felt	felt
fight	fought	fought
find	found	found
fly	flew	flown
forbid	forbade	forbidden
forget	forgot	forgotten
freeze	froze	frozen
get	got	got (US gotten)
give	gave	given
go	went	gone
grow	grew	grown
have	had	had
hear	heard	heard
hide	hid	hidden
hit	hit	hit
hold	held	held
hurt	hurt	hurt
keep	kept	kept
know	knew	known
lay	laid	laid
lead	led	led
learn	learnt	learnt
leave	left	left
lend	lent	lent
let	let	let

Stem	Past Tense	Past Participle
lie	lay	lain
lose	lost	lost
make	made	made
mean	meant	meant
meet	met	met
pay	paid	paid
quit	quit	quit
read	read	read
ride	rode	ridden
ring	rang	rung
rise	rose	risen
run	ran	run
say	said	said
see	saw	seen
sell	sold	sold
send	sent	sent
set	set	set
shake	shook	shaken
shoot	shot	shot
show	showed	shown
shut	shut	shut
sing	sang	sung
sit	sat	sat
sleep	slept	slept
speak	spoke	spoken
spend	spent	spent
split	split	split
spread	spread	spread
stand	stood	stood
steal	stole	stolen
stick	stuck	stuck
swim	swam	swum
take	took	taken
teach	taught	taught
tear	tore	torn
tell	told	told
think	thought	thought
throw	threw	thrown
understand	understood	understood
wear	wore	worn
win	won	won
withdraw	withdrew	withdrawn
write	wrote	written

Glossary

abroad in or to a foreign country

to **acquire** to buy – Also, an **acquisition**

advertisement publicity designed to sell a product or service – Also, to **advertise**; **advertising** Abbreviations: **advert**; **ad.**

to **adapt** to make something suitable for a new use (*It takes time to adapt to living abroad.*)

to **adopt** to take and use something (*All his suggestions were adopted.*)

to **afford** to be able to do something because you have enough time or money (*We can't afford to buy it; it's too expensive.*)

an **agenda** a list of things to discuss at a meeting

an **agent** a person or company that represents the interests of another company in a market – Also, **agency**

to **allocate** to decide to use something for a particular purpose (*We've allocated 20 seats to the press.*)

annoyed a little angry, irritated

ASAP Abbreviation for 'As Soon As Possible'

assets the things a company has or owns, including property, plant, equipment, stocks, money in the bank and money owed by customers – Opposite = **liabilities**

to **assist** to help – Also, an **assistant**

atmosphere the mood or feeling of a place

ATTN Abbreviation: attention or for the attention of

an **auditorium** the part of a theatre, hall, etc. where the audience sits

to **authorize** to give official permission for something

to **automate** to make something operate by machine, without needing people – Also, **automation**

autonomy the right to control your own affairs

to **avoid** to keep away from something or somebody, to prevent something happening (*We want to avoid accidents.*)

a **balance sheet** a statement of the financial position of a company at a particular time, balancing what it has against what it owes

to **ban** to forbid something officially

bankrupt not having enough money to pay your debts (*The company went bankrupt, owing millions of pounds.*)

a **bar code** a series of lines printed on a product that can be read by machine to give a price or reference number

a **battery** a device which provides electricity for a car, radio, etc.

to **bear with someone** to wait for someone without complaining (*Could you bear with me a second while I get a pen.*)

Big Blue The nickname of IBM, the computer company

to **blame** to think or say that somebody is responsible for something bad that has happened (*Don't blame me for the delay. It wasn't my fault.*)

bn Abbreviation for billion (*FFr 3.7bn*)

a **board** a group of people who control an organization or company

a **bonus** an extra sum of money paid to an employee

to **book** to make a reservation (*I'd like to book a room for two nights.*)

to **borrow** to take something from someone that you intend to give back

a **brand** a particular make of goods, or their trademark

a **breakdown of costs** a description of each separate cost

to **bribe** to give money to someone in order to persuade them to do something dishonest – Also, a **bribe**

a **broadsheet** a 'quality' newspaper printed on large sheets of paper

a **brochure** a small book with pictures designed to sell products

to **budge** to move

a **budget** an amount of money set aside for a special purpose (*The advertising budget*); a financial plan showing how much money a company intends to make and spend – Also, to **budget**

bulk the large size or amount of something (*We can get a bigger discount if we buy in bulk.*)

bungee jumping a sport where people are attached to a spring before jumping from high places

bureaucracy the system of official rules that a large organization might have – Also, **bureaucratic**

a **candidate** a person who applies for a job or wants to be elected

capital a sum of money used to start a business – Also, **capital expenditure** = money spent on buildings, equipment, etc.

carriage the cost of transporting goods from one place to another

cash money that is ready to spend, in notes and coins or (for a company) in a bank account

cc [= 'carbon copy'] used in memos and letters to say they are also being sent to other people

a **channel** a way or route along which something travels (*communication channels; distribution channels*)

a **circulation** the number of newspapers, magazines, etc. that are sold each time it is produced

to **claim** to ask for something you think you should have – Also, a **claim** (*an insurance claim; a pay claim*)

to **co-ordinate** to organize different things or people so they can work together efficiently

a **code** a group of numbers used to identify something (*I need to phone the Spanish office; what's the code for Madrid?*)

to **come up** to happen unexpectedly

a **commission** money you get for selling things (*The agent wants a 10% commission.*)

competent able to do a job, having the necessary skill – Opposite = **incompetent**

a **competitor** another company operating in the same area of the market – Also, to **compete**; **competition**; **competitive**

complimentary free (*Complimentary tickets = tickets you needn't pay for*)

to **compromise** to change a negotiating position in order to reach an agreement – Also, a **compromising position** = a situation where people think you have behaved dishonestly

a **concession** something you agree to do in order to end an argument

to **conflict** to disagree with (*The two reports conflicted with each other.*) – Also, a conflict

to **consume** to use (*The US imports 45% of the oil it consumes.*) – Also, a **consumer**; **consumption**

convenient fitting in well with people's needs or plans; causing no problems (*Would 3.30 be convenient?*) – Opposite = **inconvenient**

a **counterfoil** a part of a cheque or receipt that you keep as a record

credit the system of buying goods or services and not paying for them until later (*We can give you 30 days credit.*) – Also, a **credit period**; a **creditor**

currency the money system of a country (*The currency of Japan is the yen.*)

dear expensive

a **deficit** the amount by which a sum of money is too small (*We have £1m and we need £3m – that's a deficit of £2m.*)

a **delivery note** a document sent to a customer along with goods, giving details of the goods

demography the study of statistics of births, deaths, marriages, etc. to show the state of a community – Also, **demographic**

to **deny** to state that something is not true (*He denied that he had told lies.*)

a **department** a section of a company often related to function (*Personnel department; Sales department*) – Abbreviation = **Dept**

to **depreciate** to lose value as a result of use or age – Also, **depreciation**

a **deputy** The second most important person in an organization (*The deputy does the work of his/her boss if the boss is absent.*)

to **devalue** to reduce the value of a currency in relation to other currencies – Also, **devaluation**

to **dial** to push the buttons on a telephone in order to call a number – Also, a **dial**

diesel the heavy oil that is used in the engines of buses, trains, and some cars

to **diminish** to get or to make something smaller or less important

direct taxation the tax you pay directly to the government, for example, income tax – Also, **indirect taxation,** for example, VAT

a **discount** a price reduction

to **disembark** to get off a plane or boat

to **dismiss** to fire, to sack, to stop employing someone

to **dispatch** to send out (*All orders are dispatched within seven days.*)

a **dispute** a disagreement or argument between people – Also, to **dispute** (*an invoice*)

to **distribute** to send goods into a market – Also, **distribution**; a **distributor**

a **division** a section of a company, often related to geographical area or product group (*The Canadian division, the plastics division*) – Abbreviation: **Div.**

DM Abbreviation for deutschmark, the currency of Germany (*DM 56*)

to **doubt** to feel uncertain about something (*I doubt if we'll finish on time.*)

dramatic sudden, very large – Also, **dramatically**

eccentric strange or unusual (*He wasn't mad; he was just a little eccentric.*)

ecology the relations between living things and their surroundings

economical saving money (*Get a smaller car – it's more economical.*)

an **economy** the operation of a country's money supply, trade, and industry – Also, **economic** (*The government's economic policy*)

efficient working well and quickly, producing a good result in the minimum time – Opposite = **inefficient**

to **emit** to send out something, for example, smoke, signals, heat – Also, **emissions**

to **employ** to give work to someone – Also, **employer** (= the company); the **employee** (= the worker); **employment; employed; unemployment; unemployed**

to **enable** to make something possible

to **encourage** to give hope, support, or confidence to somebody

encs Abbreviation for 'enclosures' – used in letters to indicate extra documents are being sent in the same envelope

to **enhance** to make better, to improve

to **enquire** to ask questions, to get information – Also, an **enquiry**; a **letter of enquiry**

an **entrepreneur** a person who starts or runs a business activity that involves risk – Also, **entrepreneurial**

environment the natural world in which people, animals, and plants live

equity the part of a company's capital that is raised through selling shares

to **estimate** to guess the cost, size, etc. of something before you have all the exact figures – Also, a **price estimate** = a written statement from a supplier giving a price for a job

expenditure money spent on something (*Government expenditure on education is very low.*)

expenses money spent for a particular purpose (*You can claim your travel expenses.*)

expertise special knowledge or skill

an **extension** a telephone that is connected to a switchboard in a large office building (*'Extension 386, please.'*)

faint quiet, not strong

fault a defect or mistake; responsibility for a mistake (*It's not my fault we're late; I was ready on time.*) – Also, **faulty** (= defective)

feasible possible to do, workable (*This plan isn't feasible; it'll take too long.*)

financial connected with money (*financial difficulties; a financial centre*)

to **fire** to dismiss, to sack, to stop employing someone

fizzy used to describe a drink containing many small bubbles; gassy

flexible can change or be changed in order to suit different situations (*flexible payment terms*)

fluorescent shining with a particular kind of hard white light

to **fluctuate** to change, to go up and down

a **franchise** official permission to sell a company's goods or services in a specified area – Also, to **franchise**

Freephone a telephone line where the receiver pays, not the caller

freight the cost of transporting goods

FFr Abbreviation for French Francs

to **fund** to supply the money for a project – Also, **funds; funding**

to **gamble** to take a risk, to bet – Also, a **gamble**

to **get in touch** to make contact (*I'll get in touch with you next week.*)

gifted talented, possessing special skills

gradual small and not sudden – Also, **gradually**

a **graduate** a person who has a degree from a university – Also, to **graduate**

grateful thankful

gross before anything is taken away, for example, **gross profit** = profit before tax – Opposite = **net**

to **grow** to increase in size or number – Also, **growth**

to **guess** to estimate, to attempt to give the right answer when you are not sure what it is

to **hack** to use a computer to access information on another computer – Also, a **hacker** = a person who hacks

to **hand in your notice** to state officially that you intend to leave a job

hands on practical experience gained by doing something

a **head-hunter** a person or company that recruits top managers from other companies

headquarters head office – Abbreviation = HQ (* *Notice headquarters is always plural*)

a **helmet** a protective head covering, metal hat

to **hesitate** to pause before doing something

a **hierarchy** an organization that has many ranks from the lowest to the highest – Also, **hierarchical**

a **hippy** a person who doesn't share the same ideas and values as most people in society – The hippy movement first appeared in the 1960s amongst young people who had long hair and colourful clothes.

to **hire** to rent something; to employ someone's services temporarily

to **ignore** to pay no attention to something

to **implement** to start using a plan or system; to put a plan into action

to **improve** to make or get better – Also, **improvement**

income money received as payment for work

to **incur** to cause or suffer something unpleasant (*We've incurred a lot of debts.*)

inflation the general increase in the price of goods and services

to **install** to put in place (*The job will be easier when the new computer is installed .*) – Also, **installation**

interest money charged (for example, by a bank) for borrowing money

inventory stocks of goods or raw materials

an **invoice** a list of goods sold with a request for payment

to **issue** to publish and give something (*We've sent the goods but we haven't issued the invoice yet.*)

IT Abbreviation for *Information Technology* – any form of technology incorporating computing, telecommunications, electronics, and broadcasting, used by people to handle information

jet lag the tired feeling you can get when you travel to a place where the local time is different

a **joint venture** a co-operative operation between two companies sharing expertise, resources, etc.

key main, important (*What are the key facts?*)

know-how practical knowledge or skill

to **lack** to have to little or none of something (*We lack the manpower we need for this job.*)

to **launch** to introduce a product to a market

a **lawyer** a person who has studied law and gives advice on legal matters

legal connected with the law (*Legal department*); allowed by law – Opposite = **illegal**

to **lend** to allow somebody to use something for fixed period of time (*If you need money, I can lend you £20.*)

liabilities debts, money a company owes to suppliers, shareholders, banks, etc. – Opposite = **assets**

a **lift** a ride in your car (*Shall I give you a lift to the station?*); an elevator

likely probable – Opposite = **unlikely**

a **limit** a restriction, a point or line that mustn't be passed (*What's the speed limit on this road?*) – Also, to **limit**

a **lorry** a large motor vehicle for carrying goods (US = a **truck**)

a **loss** the money lost by a business: total sales minus total costs (if this figure is negative)

m Abbreviation for million

a **margin** the difference between the cost price and the selling price (*We're operating on tight (i.e., small) margins.*)

a **mark-up** an increase in price, the percentage of the cost price you add to give the selling price for goods

a **memo** a note sent from one person to another within an organization – Formal = a memorandum

to **misspell** to spell wrongly

momentum pace, speed (*The recovery is gaining momentum.*)

to **motivate** to make people want to do things by making them interesting – Also, **motivation; motivator**

negligible extremely small, hardly noticeable – Also, **negligibly**

negotiate to bargain, to discuss a business deal or contract, to reach an agreement by discussion – Also, **negotiation; negotiator**

to **network** to connect computers together

a **niche** market a small but significant part of the total market

off cancelled (*The meeting is off; she can't make it.*)

an **option** a choice, an alternative

to **oust** to remove somebody from a position or job

to **outdo** to do something better than another person

to **outnumber** to be greater in number (*People in favour of the motion outnumbered those against it two to one.*)

output The quantity of goods produced (*We can't increase output without more machines.*)

to **outweigh** to be more important (*The advantages outweigh the disadvantages.*)

an **overdraft** a bank facility that allows you to withdraw more money than you have in an account

to **owe** to be in debt (*We borrowed £5m and we've paid back £3m but we still owe £2m.*)

PDQ Abbreviation for 'Pretty Damn Quick'

a **peak** a high point on a graph – Opposite = a **trough** – Also, to **peak**

a **penalty** a punishment for breaking a law or rule

a **pension** money that is paid regularly to someone who has retired – Also, a **pensioner** = the person

to **persecute** to cause somebody to suffer – Also, **persecution**

petrol fuel used in motor vehicles

pharmaceutical connected with the production of medicine and drugs

a **pity** something that makes you feel sad or disappointed (*It's a pity you have to leave so soon.*)

(a) **plant** a factory or the machinery that is in a factory

a **platform** the place where you get on and off trains in a station

pls Abbreviation for 'please' – might be used in e-mail messages, telexes, and notes

to **plunge** to move downwards suddenly

to **pollute** to make air, rivers, etc. dirty (*The river was polluted by waste chemicals.*) – Also, **pollution**

potential something that may happen, undeveloped qualities (*This market has great potential for future growth .*)

pp used before signatures in letters when another person has signed in the writer's absence

prejudice a strong feeling of like or dislike that is not based on experience or reason

prestigious respected or admired

productive useful, producing in large quantities – Also, **productivity** (*More efficient methods will lead to greater productivity.*)

a **profit** the money made by a business – Also, **profitable** = making a profit; a **profit and loss account** = a company's trading figures, usually for a one year period; a **profit centre** = a unit within an organization which keeps separate accounts and should make a profit

a **projection** a guess about a future amount based on information available at present (*Sales projections for the next five years*)

a **prototype** the first model or design, which will be modified and developed

to **purchase** to buy

qualified having the right education, diplomas and experience for a job – Also, a **qualification**

to **query** to question something because you think there has been a mistake (*The bill is rather high; you'd better query it.*) – Also, **queries** = questions

to **quote** to give a price estimate – Also, a **quotation**

a **range** a group of products sold by one company

rapid very fast – Also, **rapidly**

a **rate** how fast something happens (*the rate of inflation*) or the level of something (*interest rates, the rate of unemployment*)

re Abbreviation for 'with reference to'

to **realize** to become fully aware of (*I didn't realize you were from Canada.*); to change plans into reality

a **receipt** a document showing you have paid for something

a **recession** a decline in economic activity (*This recession is worse than the one we had in the seventies.*)

to **recover** to get better after a difficult period – Also, a **recovery**

to **recruit** to employ or take on new staff – Also, **recruitment**

to **recycle** to treat used material so it can be used again (*Recycled paper*)

redundant no longer needed, dismissed, without work (*They have made 400 workers redundant because of the recession.*) – Also, **redundancies** = job losses

to **refund** to pay back money spent (*Save the receipts and we'll refund your expenses.*) – Also, a **refund**

reliable consistently good in quality, performance or work – Opposite = **unreliable**

a **reminder** a letter sent to remind customers about unpaid invoices

to **rent** to hire, to borrow something in return for money – Also, **rent** = the money paid to rent something

to **resign** to give up or leave a job

a **retail outlet** a place where goods are sold to the public, for example a shop or supermarket

to **retire** to stop working at the end of a career, usually between the ages of 60 and 65 – Also, **retirement**

revenue income received by a government, company, etc.

RGDS Abbreviation for 'REGARDS' – sometimes used at the end of telexes

a **risk** something that might cause danger – Also, **risky** (*A risky investment*)

a **royalty** an amount of money paid to a franchise company by a franchisee

to **sack** to dismiss, to fire, to stop employing someone

a **salary** a monthly payment for doing a job

sale or return a system where retailers can return goods to their supplier if they fail to sell them

a **sample** a specimen, small quantities of a product that show what the rest is like; a small number of people who are asked questions in a survey in order to get information about a larger group

scarce in short supply – Opposite = plentiful

scope The chance or opportunity to do something (*There's scope for improvement.*)

to **second** to move somebody from their job to another for a fixed period of time

a **sector** a part of the economy of a country (*The manufacturing sector*)

a **segment** a section of a market

a **share** a part, a fraction (*We have increased our market share by 2%.*); a part of a company (*With 51% of the shares we control the company.*) – Also, a **shareholder** = a person who owns shares

short-sighted not seeing what will happen in the future

a **shot** a TV advertisement

to **shrink** to get smaller – Also, **shrinkage** = loss of stock in a shop through theft

simultaneous happening at exactly the same time

a **sketch** a simple quick drawing without many details

to **slump** to fall suddenly and by a large amount

to **soar** to rise very fast

a **socket** a hole in which something fits (*A socket for an electric light bulb*)

specifications details and instructions describing design and materials (*product specifications; building specifications*)

to **sponsor** to help to pay for a special event, for example a sports event or a charity football tournament – Also, **sponsorship**

staff all the people who work for a company: its personnel, its employees

a **stake** a number of shares in a company

to **stall** to delay

status your social or professional position in relation to other people (*Teachers don't have a high status in this country.*)

stock goods in storage waiting to be sold; a share in the capital of a company

a **stockbroker** a person who trades in stocks and shares

to **streamline** to make an organization or process work better by making it simpler and more efficient

a **strike** the organized stopping of work by employees as a result of a dispute

a **subordinate** a person with a lower rank or position

a **subsidiary** a company that is controlled by another company

substantial large – Also, **substantially**

to **supply** to provide customers with goods or services – Also, a **supplier**

a **survey** an investigation made by asking a group of people about their opinions or behaviour

to **survive** to continue to live

a **tabloid** a 'popular' newspaper printed on small sheets of paper

to **tackle** to deal with something difficult, for example a problem

a **target** a result you want, a goal, an objective – Also, to **target** = to aim at something

a **tenant** a person or company that pays rent for rooms, offices, etc., so that they can use them

a **till** a cash register, a machine where money is kept in a shop

a **tip** a piece of advice; money given to a taxi driver, waitress, etc. to thank them – Also, to **tip**

TLX abbreviation for 'telex'

TNKS abbreviation for 'thanks' – might be used in an e-mail message or telex

TQM abbreviation for 'Total Quality Management'

to **trigger** to cause something to start (*The cigarette smoke triggered the fire alarms.*)

a **trough** a low point on a graph – Opposite = a peak

to **tumble** to fall suddenly in an uncontrolled way

turbulence disturbance; violent and uneven movement

turnover the total sales of a company – Also, **staff turnover** = the rate of staff leaving and joining a company

to **upgrade** to change something so it is a higher standard (*Can I upgrade this ticket to first class?*)

VAT abbreviation for 'Value Added Tax'

a **venue** the place where a conference, sports match, etc. happens

to **vibrate** to move quickly from side to side – Also, **vibration**

a **volunteer** a person who offers or agrees to do something without being forced or paid to do it – Also, to **volunteer**

wages a weekly payment for doing a job, usually paid to manual workers

to **weaken** to become weaker

a **workaholic** someone who works too hard; someone addicted to their job

a **work-load** an amount of work to be done (*We have a heavy work-load.*)

a **worksheet** a document for recording work that is in progress or completed

¥ abbreviation for Yen – the currency of Japan

zaniness craziness, madness

191

Oxford University Press
Great Clarendon Street, Oxford OX2 6DP

Oxford   New York
Athens Auckland Bangkok Bogotá Buenos Aires Cape Town
Chennai Dar es Salaam Delhi Florence Hong Kong Istanbul Karachi
Kolkata Kuala Lumpur Madrid Melbourne Mexico City Mumbai Nairobi
Paris São Paulo Shanghai Singapore Taipei Tokyo Toronto Warsaw

with associated companies in
Berlin Ibadan

OXFORD and OXFORD ENGLISH are trade marks of Oxford University Press

ISBN 0 19 452028 5 International Edition
ISBN 0 19 451398 x German Edition
Bestellnummer: 37509

© Oxford University Press 1994

First Published in the International Edition 1994
Fourteenth impression 2001

First published in the German Edition 1997
Fourth impression 2000

No unauthorized photocopying

*The publishers would like to thank the following for their permission to
reproduce photographs:*
Ace Library: p. 46, (man and woman in shop); Air France: p. 71, (logo);
Art Directors: pp. 46, (woman on computer, man on computer, computer
software), 74, (visitors), 84, (designing), 106, (power station),130,
(business meeting); Bard Martin Photography/AT & T Telephone
Company: p. 27, (teleticket); Barrett Rudich: p. 6, (company employees);
BDM: p. 87; Bob Thomas Sports: p. 129, (Steve Coppell); Body Shop: p. 88;
British Rail/Intercity: (logo); Budget: p. 71, (logo); Business Age
Magazine: p. 65; J Allan Cash Library: pp. 80, (friends sharing corn wine),
106, (turbo alternator); Detroit Edison: p. 86; Dick Beach/Stakis Group: p.
136, (Dick Beach); Ecoscene: p. 38, (solar power station, bottle bank,
petrol station); Sally & Richard Greenhill: p. 80, (muslim women
washing); Greenpeace: p. 38, (power station, recycling centre); Helena
Rubeinstein: p. 24; Hertz UK: p. 71, (logo); Holiday Inn Worldwide: p. 71,
(logo); Impact Photos/Julian Calder: p. 10, (Richard Branson); Itochu
Corporation: p. 6 (Minoru Murofushi); L'Oréal: p. 24; Laura Ashley: p.
104; The Lego Group: pp. 53, 54; Lynda King Taylor/Liz Mason: p. 136
(Lynda King Taylor); MicroWarehouse Inc: p. 72; Minnesota Power: p. 6,
(Lisa Schadewald); Network Library: p. 141, (newspaper vendor,
newspaper stall); Nicholas Brealey Publishing: p. 37; Nikwax: p. 115;
Pernod Ricard Group: p. 6, (Bernard Cazals); Peter Sibbald Photography/
Microsoft: p. 33; Photographers Library: p. 118; Rex Features: pp. 10,
(Richard Branson), 156, (Robert Maxwell); Robert Bosch UK Ltd: p. 27,
(DIY power tools); Sheraton Hotel: p. 71, (logo); SNCF: p. 71, (logo);
Softbank Corporation: pp. 47, 50; Steve Coppell: p. 129; Telegraph
Colour Library: p. 80, (Arabs meeting); Tony Stone: pp. 46, (computer),
72, (construction site), 84, (road construction, construction platforms,
construction engineer), 106, (jet engine assembly, business woman, car
engine assembly); Trip Library/R Chester: p. 66, p. 80, (Indian greeting),
130, (meeting in Calcutta); Tropix: p. 80, (two men shaking hands); Veba:
p. 6, (Anke Rohland)

Illustrations by:
Veronica Bailey: p. 34; Shirley Barker: p. 17; John Barrett: unit opener
artwork; Ken Binder: p. 42; John Gilkes; Steve Fricker: pp. 56, 125; Martin
Hargreaves: p. 13; David Loftus: pp. 28, 114, 139; Nigel Paige: pp. 19, 21,
40, 73, 77, 79, 94, 112, 145, 146; Colin Salmon: p. 22; Tim Slade: pp. 26,
81; David Williams: p. 82.

Studio Photography by:
Mark Mason: p. 141, (newspapers)

Design by
Shireen Nathoo Design

Acknowledgements

*The author and publisher would like to thank the following for
permission to use adapted material and/or to reproduce copyright
material:*
Air France, New York: extracts from sponsored essays published in
Fortune magazine, 1992; Laura Ashley Ltd; BDM Technologies Inc.:
advertisement; The Body Shop International PLC; Nicholas Brealey
Publishing, London: extracts from John Mole: Mind your Manners —
Managing Culture Clash in the Single European Market, © John Mole,
1990, 1992; Business Magazines UK Ltd: extract from article in
Management Week, 1991; Detroit Edison; *The Economist*: graphs; The
Economist Books: graphs from *The Economist Book of Vital World
Statistics: a Complete Guide to the World in Figures*, Copyright © 1990
The Economist Books; The European/Syndication International: table from
The European, 6.8.91, extracts from article in *The European*, 5.3.92;
Guardian Newspapers Ltd: extracts from article by Susan Thomas © *The
Guardian* 1993; Haymarket Motoring Magazines: extracts from chart in
What Car?; The Lego Group; L'Oréal; MacWarehouse; *Management
Today*: text adapted from 'Micro Myopia', February 1992; Mintel
International Group Ltd: statistics from 'Regional Newspapers' report,
March 1992; Mori Ltd: survey data, 1987; Nestlé SA; Newspaper Publishing
PLC: extracts from articles by Lynda King Taylor and Dick Beach from *The
Independent on Sunday*; and MacDonalds graph from *The Independent;*
Oxford University Press: extract from *The Oxford Wordpower Dictionary*,
1993; P-E International/Times Newspapers Ltd: graph from The Times, ©
Times Newspapers, 1992; The Procter & Gamble Company: extracts from
brochure 'Total Quality Environmental Management' © Proctor & Gamble
1993; Reader's Digest Ltd: table; Rosters Ltd: Job quiz extract from Susan
Clemie and Dr. John Nicholson: The Good Interview Guide, ed. Rosemary
Burr, (Rosters 1991). Daniel Sarberg and Schering SA; Softbank
Corporation; The Telegraph PLC: extracts from article in *The Daily
Telegraph*, London, 1993; Text 100 Ltd on behalf of Microsoft
Corporation; Virgin Group of companies.
Product copy and photographs from the MacWAREHOUSE catalog are
copyrighted © 1993 by Micro WAREHOUSE, Inc., 47 Water Street, South
Norwalk, Connecticut 06854, and are reprinted with permission.
"MACWAREHOUSE" is a registered trademark of Micro Warehouse, Inc.
Product names and box covers are trademarks and copyrights of the
respective software publishers.

Although every effort has been made to trace and contact copyright
holders before publication, this has not always been possible. If notified,
the publisher will be pleased to rectify any errors or omissions at the
earliest opportunity.

The author would like to thank the many friends, relatives, colleagues
acquaintances, students, and English teachers who have helped in writing
this book. Special thanks to Rick Baldwin for his superb resources bank,
Robert Gibson for his 'negotiating tips', Emma Tanner for her practical
ideas, Emma Wood for her pronunciation know-how, and Michael Black
for his steadfast support. I'm also grateful for the valuable advice I
received from EF International School of English, Cambridge where these
materials were first piloted. Many thanks also to Barnaby Newbolt and his
excellent editorial team for their inspiration and good humour when I
changed things for the umpteenth time. And last, but by no means least,
I'd like to thank my family, Brian, Georgie, and Tom, for their patience
and tolerance.

The author and editors would like to thank the following institutions and
individuals who helped us by piloting and commenting on the material in
this course during its preparation. Many people not listed here also
helped us with editorial research of various kinds which we carried out
during the past year; we are extremely grateful to them all.
Infolangues, Lyon; Interlang, Madrid; International House, Bilbao;
Lacunza, San Sebastian; Lanser, Bilbao; LinguaSec, Madrid; Logos,
Grenoble; Lyon Langues, Lyon.
Margaret Allavoine, Alison Barcley, Karen Carnet, Madame Chambon,
Jean-Claude Châtaignier, Patrcia Dadswell, Elizabeth Davenel, Catherine
Delhomme, Lori Dovidio Dabbagh, Mavis Etienne, Phil Eyre, Josephine
Ezzarouali, Jane Frugère, Michael Frankel, Janey Futerill, Simon Gardner,
Joanna Gates, Kim Griffin, François Guiselin, Josiane Hay, Guy Heath,
Thomas Kaelin, Elizabeth Labouteley, Christiane Laupies, Patricia
Matthiae-Buisson, Robert Meillier, Dominique Mondoulet, Sylvie Monin,
Alexandra Neasham-Laforcade, Sally Nichols, Raquel de Nicolás, Susan
Pruvot, Jean-Philippe Pays, Anne Siegmann, Sylvie Staub, Wendy Stewart,
Jeremy Townend, Alfred Weber, Geoffrey Williams, Janet Wilson-Smith,
Tessa Wisely.